The Inside Passage

Along the Wild Pacific Coast from Seattle to Alaska • Bernd Römmelt

The Inside Passage

⊁B BUCHER

CONTENTS

A First Approach

Aho, said Yeil, the wise man. Come closer. I have a story to tell.
Rustling his feathers, he whispers, I shall tell you a story of how
this place began. Leaping into the air, transforming into Raven,
he flies to the treetop. Come, my people, and I will lead you to a
far-off place. Here, under the glacier, there is an ice passage.
It is waiting for you.

Robert Willard Jr. (Raven/Beaver Clan Elder)
from the Tlingit people

North America's Most Scenic Voyage

August 1997. I was sitting in front of my little log cabin on the shores of Anan Bay in southeast Alaska. Three days had passed since Eric, my guide, had set me down here. I wanted to photograph bears fishing for salmon in the dark rainforest. Fog had descended over the little bay. I put the water on to make some coffee. It was still cold. It had rained almost continuously for the past two weeks. I like rain, but after such a long period it starts to affect your spirits. Today was the first clear, sunny day. I screwed up my eyes as I looked out across the bay. The call of the wild rang out high above my head: a young bald eagle was sitting in the crown of a mighty Sitka spruce, squawking for its parents. I get goose-pimples whenever I hear the sound. Suddenly I heard the sound of cracking twigs in the undergrowth: it was a female brown bear with her two cubs. Just twenty meters (22 yards) away from me they walked along the beach, upturning stones and gambolling around. The three bears were not in the least concerned at my presence. I continued to sit quietly. With almost fifteen years of experience of bears I knew that the situation was not dangerous. I watched the family for a short while longer until they disappeared into the dense rainforest …

Even today, I can still remember exactly how I felt at the time. The region is a paradise – one of the last on Earth. I regarded myself as privileged to be able to experience it all in this way. I was overcome with a feeling of deep closeness with my surroundings. I spent three weeks there on that occasion – the start of a great love affair.

In the winter of 2005 I was commissioned to take the photographs for a book about the Inside Passage. I could hardly believe my good fortune. But my initial euphoria was rapidly followed by disillusionment. A book about the entire Inside Passage – an almost impossible task, I thought.

A glance at the map indicated the scale of the project: The Inside Passage stretches along the coast from Seattle in the US state of Washington northwards as far as Skagway in Alaska. Parts of the coastline of two US states, Washington und Alaska, and the Canadian province of British Columbia belong to the region. It is 1,050 nautical miles from Seattle in the south to Skagway in the north. If you were to trace the length of the entire coastline, including all the bays of the mainland and the coast of all the islands, you would travel almost 40,000 kilometers (25,000 miles) – the equivalent of a journey around the world! And yet …

In July 2005 I started work. Until summer 2007 I spent almost five months on the Northwest coast of North America, spent days watching bears catching salmon, spent others surrounded by hundreds of bald eagles, saw killer whales leap into the air right beside me, watched humpback whales surfacing with their jaws wide open, observed glaciers break off into the sea – and felt as if I was gradually growing webbed fingers. I cursed the long periods of rain when there was not a single ray of sunshine for weeks on end, and I felt as if I had been born again as I finally revelled in the first warming rays. No other region on Earth has enchanted me like the coastal region of the Inside Passage. I can see it all again before me as I write: the glaciers, the people, the smell of the sea, the white black bears …

The Inside Passage, this labyrinth of islands and bays, is one of the loveliest and most varied coastal regions in the world. Here you will find the last extensive areas of temperate rainforest,

Left: On the few clear days there is a spectacular view of the Gastineau Channel and the surrounding Coast Mountains from Mount Roberts, the mountain which rises up outside Juneau.

Bottom: Heavy, persistent rain transforms even tiny mountain streams into raging torrents.

Right below: In the Chilkat Valley, two bald eagles wait patiently for the feast to begin in early November. As fall draws to a close a late salmon migration attracts up to three thousand bald eagles to the Chilkat River near Haines.

countless calving glaciers and craggy mountains more than 2,000 meters (6,560 feet) high. Here, too, you will encounter a unique fauna: in its food-rich waters live sea otters, seals, sea lions, orcas, various species of dolphin, humpback whales, countless species of salmon, and herrings. The creatures which live on land include the wolf, brown and black bears, Kermode bears, wolverines, groundhogs, Arctic goats, elks and porcupines. The Inside Passage is home to countless species of bird, including the

heraldic bird of the USA, the bald eagle, and the red-throated diver, the lovely grey heron, the comical puffin, and the kingfisher.

For thousands of years the Northwest Coastal Indians, the most highly developed indigenous culture of North America, has been settled here. Their totem poles are world famous and can still be seen virtually everywhere. In addition to the unspoilt wilderness the visitor will find cosmopolitan cities like Seattle and Vancouver, Victoria and Juneau.

Geography

A bird's eye view of the Inside Passage reveals three geographical factors which characterize the landscape: the coastal mountains of the mainland, the pattern of offshore islands and the high mountains on Vancouver Island, the Queen Charlotte Islands and the Alexander Archipelago.

The massive coastal mountains on the mainland, which extend along the entire coast from Seattle to Skagway, were formed across the millennia where the Pacific and the North American tectonic plates meet. The tensions which arise along the edges of the plates can still be felt today. Earthquakes are almost a daily occurrence, even though most of them are relatively minor. The southern regions of the Inside Passage belong to the so-called "Ring of Fire", the arc of volcanoes extending from the western Aleutian Islands as far as California. The major eruption of Mount St. Helen's in

Washington State in 1980 provided the local inhabitants with a painful reminder of the hot spot on which they had settled. Wind, weather, glaciers and, of course, the sea have also helped to form the Inside Passage.

Climate

Apart from the Pacific Ocean, it is the mountains of the mainland which are mainly responsible for the damp climate that defines the Inside Passage. Over 2,500 meters (8,200 feet) high, these mighty peaks represent an almost insuperable barrier for the clouds which gather above the Pacific. The clouds pile up on the mountains and it starts raining – or snowing in winter – for days, sometimes for weeks on end. Of course there are considerable differences in rainfall and climate along the length of the coastline which extends over one thousand nautical miles (approx. 1800 kilometers). For example, the San Juan Islands near Seattle in

Top left: The little fishing boat looks almost lost against the backdrop of the Coast Mountains, plunging steeply down towards the sea.
Top right: An orca family patrols the coast of the Johnstone Strait, one of the best places in the world to observe killer whales.
Below right and bottom left: South Sawyer Glacier at the end of Tracy Arm affords a breathtaking natural spectacle. A explosion can be heard as part of the tongue of the glacier breaks off into the sea. The entire bay is filled with sparkling blocks of ice.

the south enjoy many more sunny days than the Alexander Archipelago in southeast Alaska. Even on the coast of southeast Alaska there are marked differences in the amount of precipitation. In Skagway, for example, the average annual rainfall is only 660 millimeters (26 inches). A little further to the south, in the region around Ketchikan, there is six times as much.

The Rainforest

The large amounts of rainfall were responsible for the growth of the temperate or cool rainforest, which, along with the glaciers and the mountains, determines not only the landscape but also the lifestyle of the inhabitants of the Inside Passage. The warm waters of the Pacific Ocean result in relatively mild temperatures almost all the year round. That is why, even in winter, most of the precipitation falls as rain. Only in the far north along the coast, in southeast Alaska near Haines and Skagway, does the winter regularly provide lower temperatures and large amounts of snow.

A typical characteristic of the temperate rainforest is the absence of large temperature differences. Throughout the entire Pacific Northwest it is hardly ever really warm, but also seldom very cold. Low-lying clouds are typical for the region and result in a mysterious, almost mystic atmosphere which immediately fascinates anyone who has ever gone for a walk in the rainforest.

With an annual rainfall of at least 2000 millimeters (78 inches), the ground remains cold and damp, even in summer. This constant dampness encourages the growth of vegetation. The forests are often impenetrable. Scarcely a ray of sunlight manages to reach the forest floor. The trees, which can live for over one thousand years, are covered with large-leaved ferns,

mosses and lichens. In the temperate rainforests of British Columbia and Alaska you will find some of the world's tallest trees. Sitka spruce, red and yellow cedar, Douglas fir and the Western hemlock are the typical forest species.

For a long time these impenetrable woods were almost untouched, so that a wealth of flora and fauna could evolve here. While in other regions of North America many species of animal have become extinct or at least decimated, the forests of British Columbia and southeast Alaska provided a last refuge for many of them. Today, fifty per cent of all the brown bears in Canada live in British Columbia, many of them in the coastal forests.

Unfortunately these last bastions of untouched Nature are threatened too. The timber industry has long had its eye on the region and is trying with all the means at its disposal to exploit the last great temperate rainforests of North America: with catastrophic results for man and beast.

History and Settlement

Nobody knows for certain exactly when the first humans settled in the region of the Inside Passage. Most experts assume, however, that the first people arrived here approximately 10,000 to 12,000 years ago, and that they arrived from the north via the Bering land bridge. As the glaciers retreated they continued to head in a southerly direction and reached the coastal regions of Alaska and British Columbia. However, several thousand years were to pass before the land was sufficiently ice-free and thus permanently habitable for a larger group of humans who could produce sufficient food and thus actually live there.

There is evidence to prove that the region was permanently settled some 3,000 to 4,000 years

ago. The people probably came from inland regions and followed the main rivers, such as the Fraser and the Columbia, towards the sea before gradually settling on the coastal strip and thus establishing the culture of the Indians of the northwest coast.

Previous double page: One of the highlights of any cruise is the detour into Glacier Bay. At the far end the ship sails along the edge of Margerie Glacier. Mount Fairweather (4,671 meters/ 15,321 feet) rises in the background.

Facing double page, all images: The Inside Passage is home to one of the last expanses of temperate rainforest on Earth. An average rainfall of up to 3,000 mm (117 inches) per year is normal here. The rainforest has many faces: moss-covered tree trunks, forest grounds saturated with moisture, treetops lost in the mists and – in winter – snow-capped peaks.

Development by Europeans

The first European explorers arrived off the northwest coast of North America in the mid-16th century. Sir Francis Drake sailed through these waters as early as 1579. Thirteen years later the Greek Juan de Fuca sailed along the Pacific coast as far as 48°N. The waterway which he used was later named after him. Another 150 years were to pass before the Russian Alexei Ilyich Chirikov reached and subsequently explored the coastal regions of southeast Alaska during the Second Kamchatka Expedition. During this expedition he probably sailed as far as the coast of what is now known as Prince of Wales Island. Between 1770 and 1790 there was increased contact. In 1774 the Spaniard Juan Perez reached what are now called the Queen Charlotte Islands and was the first European to describe the Pacific Northwest

coast. In 1775 Bruno de Hezeta y Dudagoitia claimed the Northwest Coast for Spain. In 1778 James Cook mapped the coastline for Great Britain and produced records about the indigenous inhabitants. Cook was followed by British and US fur traders of the legendary Hudson's Bay Company, who were soon competing with the Russians for the fur trade. During 1792/93 George Vancouver sailed along the coast of southeast Alaska in search of the Northwest Passage, and in the same year the British fur trader Alexander Mackenzie reached the Dean Channel near Bella Coola via the land route. In 1799 Alexander Baranov, a Russian, established a Russian trading post near what is now Sitka. Although the first Europeans saw themselves primarily as scientists and explorers, as the years passed the fur trade became increasingly important. As early as 1805 the first Russian merchant ship set sail from Alaska to China,

fully laden with furs. The fur traders were especially keen on the valuable sea otter furs and sealskins. The Russian, British and US merchants pursued the fur trade so aggressively that by 1825 the previously large sea otter population was severely threatened. Only a change in fashion taste in Europe saved the cute creature from total extinction. In 1843 the Hudson's Bay Company built a fort in Victoria on Vancouver Island, which was followed by increasing numbers of smaller trading posts.

Although the coastal strip of the American Northwest was highly inaccessible, increasing numbers of humans settled here. Small fishing and lumber camps were established. In 1858 gold was discovered in the Cariboo Mountains of present-day British Columbia. A regular gold rush ensued throughout the region. Timber from the coastal forests became a sought-after export commodity.

1867 was to prove a memorable year in the history of Alaska. Until then, Alaska was Russian territory, with Sitka in the southeast as the capital. The Russians then sold the apparently

Above: A fishing boat glides through the Gastineau Channel near Juneau. Clear days like this one are rare even in summer.

Top right: The ice floes from South Sawyer Glacier sparkle like diamonds as they float in Tracy Arm.

Below right: Low tide reveals a treasure trove: shells and pebbles twinkle in rainbow colours.

worthless region of Alaska to the United States for no less than US$ 7.2 million. William Seward, the American secretary of state who negotiated the agreement with the Russians, was subjected to considerable ridicule and criticism in his own country. At that time no one knew what treasures lay buried beneath the soil of Alaska: the first gold deposits were not found

until four years later. In 1871 British Columbia became Canada's fifth province. In 1878 Alaska's first fish processing plants were opened in Sitka and Klawock. John Muir, one of the few scientists and explorers whose prime aim was not the region's rich mineral resources, but his interest in the unique natural surroundings and the culture of the indigenous inhabi-

tants, travelled in 1879 through Glacier Bay with the help of a native guide. He was so fascinated by the beauty of the landscape that he began to write a diary. His observations over a period of twenty years changed the image of Alaska. Muir's travel journal lured the first tourists to southeast Alaska at the end of the 19th century.

The Canadian Pacific Railroad was completed in 1885, and increasing numbers of adventure seekers started heading west. Today's metropolises of Vancouver und Seattle grew from small settlements into major cities.

In 1897 the Northwest Coast experienced its greatest influx of people. One year previously, the gold-diggers John Carmacks, Charlie Tagish and Jim Skookum had discovered vast gold deposits in the Klondike River, a small tributary of the Yukon River in the neighboring Yukon Territory. From this point onward there was no holding the rush. Not far from the place where they had found the gold, the gold-diggers' settlement Dawson (named after the geologist George Mercer Dawson, who had explored the region) appeared almost overnight, and adventurers from all over the world headed north. In 1898, there were up to 40,000 people living in Dawson (today there are only some 1,200!). Since the Yukon Territory was not yet accessible by land, the soldiers of fortune travelled along the waterway through the pattern of islands of the Inside Passage, in order to reach at least Dyea and Skagway at the farther northern end of the Passage. From there they headed over the (in)famous Chilkoot Pass to the Canadian Yukon Territory. Hundreds of thousands of gold prospectors arrived by ship in Seattle and San Francisco but fewer than half of them reached the Klondike. The Inside Passage was the most important transport route to the north. Just three years later the bubble had burst and peace returned – a peace that would last until 1941.

The Japanese bombing of Pearl Harbor in 1941 also affected the Inside Passage. As a result the Americans built the Alaska Highway, almost

Previous double page: All day long the rain veiled Johnstone Strait in thick mist. Late that evening the sun came out and created this magical atmosphere.
Above: In spite of the heavy rainfall, southeast Alaska is a paradise for outdoor enthusiasts. Waterproof clothing is a must.
Center: A black bear has caught its prey. Now he makes off as quickly as he can before another bear grabs the delicious morsel.
Top right: As day draws to a close, what better place to experience the peace and quiet of nature than in one's own tent on a deserted beach?!

shrimp, mussels and herring are the main species which are fished. The fishing industry is currently the biggest private sector employer in southeast Alaska. It creates more jobs than oil, timber and tourism together. In 2001 more than 4.7 million tonnes of fish were caught in the sea, representing a market value of US$ 870 million. During the 1970s the so-called fish farms were set up along the coast of the Inside Passage. These fish-farming businesses were highly controversial from the beginning. Critics accused them of polluting the water and destroying the gene pool of the "wild" fish stocks.

Fish farms were banned in Alaska in 1989. However, they continue to be permitted in British Columbia and Washington State, and the controversy continues regarding this type of "fish production". Its supporters see fish farming as the only salvation for the declining fishing industry, while its opponents condemn it as mass production which poisons the seas and threatens the species in the wild.

In addition to the fishing industry, the timber industry has always been the most important source of income along the coast of the Inside Passage. For a long time the vast forest regions were regarded as a virtually inexhaustible source of raw materials. Between 1850 and 1900 the booming mining industry and the construction of the railroad led to a disproportionate demand for timber. The first large-scale sawmills and wood-processing companies were established in British Columbia and in Washington State. Due to the high transport and development costs it took a little longer in Alaska before the first big firms grew up here too at the beginning of the 20th century. There are basically five species of tree in the forests of the Inside Passage which are important for the timber industry: the Sitka spruce, the red and yellow cedar, the Douglas fir and the Western

2,300 kilometers (1438 miles) long, linking Dawson Creek in Canada with Delta Junction in Central Alaska. Alaska and the Canadian Yukon Territory were thus reachable by land for the first time. Soon the towns of Haines and Skagway were linked to the Alaska Highway network, which made the Inside Passage into a further springboard for trips to the Far North.

The Present

Apart from the main metropolises of Seattle and Vancouver, and to a certain extent also Juneau and Victoria, most people in the coastal region of the Inside Passage continue to live from fishing and/or timber. In some districts, such as Nanaimo on Vancouver Island and Bellingham in Washington State in the US, extensive coal deposits played a certain role until recently. During the 19th century the main fishing centers had developed around the three major rivers of the Inside Passage: Fraser, Skeena and Stikine. Although the fish stocks have been reduced, sometimes dramatically, during recent decades, fishing remains the principal source of income in many communities. Salmon, halibut,

Above: Sunset over Johnstone Strait.

Right: If you join the Mackays on one of their excursions from Port McNeill on Vancouver Island you may be lucky enough to see not only whales but also eagles, bears, dolphins and sea lions.

Top right: The raven is an important figure in the mythology of the Indians of the Northwest – a cultural hero and a devious character.

hemlock. Today the timber industry is caught up in a crisis. Timber prices have fallen and the pressure from environmental protection organizations is increasing. Especially in British Columbia, but also in Washington State, excessive clear cutting has radically changed the appearance of the landscape. On Vancouver Island, for example, there are virtually no mountain ridges which have been left intact. A lively dispute has arisen between environmental protectionists on the one hand and the government and the timber companies on the other, as to how the resource timber can be uti-

lized more sustainably in the future. In spite of the crisis in the timber industry, the sector remains an important economic factor. The small coastal communities in particular earn virtually their entire income from the sale of timber.

Tourism is a source of income which is of growing importance. Even during the era of the famous naturalist and the "Father of the National Parks of the United States", John Muir (1838–1914), cruise ships travelled along the Inside Passage. Tourism really got going, however, during the mid-1970s, when increasing

numbers of cruise companies started to include the Inside Passage in their programme. Estimates indicate that the passengers of the cruise ships alone spend US$ 181 million annually. Every year, the vast liners bring hundreds of thousands of tourists to the region. Alaska's capital Juneau (approx. 30,000 inhabitants) was invaded by more than 680,000 cruise passengers in 2001. Not only the countless souvenir shops profit from the visitors; so do the numerous small companies offering whale-watching tours, glacier tours, bear-watching tours or river-rafting-tours.

There is admittedly a downside to this growing tourism. For example, on some days the three or four ships which dock simultaneously in Juneau harbour envelop the town in a thick cloud of smoke. The town center is full of kitschy souvenir shops. Many smaller communities do not profit at all from the tourism, since the giant ocean liners only anchor in certain places, such as Sitka or Skagway. The cruise liners mostly start out from the cities of Seattle and Vancouver in the south.

Traveling along the Inside Passage

Anyone wishing to travel along the Inside Passage must board a ship – at least for most of the journey. There are several ways of travelling the route. One possibility is to board one of the cruise ships in Seattle or Vancouver. These ships sail through the waters of the Inside Passage, but seldom stop. And that is the problem. Because if you wish to truly experience the

Inside Passage at close quarters, to smell, experience and feel the remarkable natural surroundings, you must disembark from the ship and go ashore.

So what are the alternatives? If you are traveling by car you can explore some sections of the Inside Passage independently – at least the southern part. Car ferries depart from Seattle and Vancouver to Vancouver Island – the biggest island in Canada. From here a scenic coastal road leads up towards the north of the island. At the latest in Port Hardy, however, you will have to board one of the BC ferries in order to cross over to Prince Rupert, the most northerly town on the Inside Passage which is on Canadian soil.

Incidentally, Prince Rupert can also be reached by road via the Yellowhead Highway. If you want to continue north of Prince Rupert towards southeast Alaska you will have to transfer to another ferry system; the legendary Alaska Marine Highway System.

Previous double page: As the mist rose over Lynn Channel, the final rays of the setting sun bathed it in an almost otherworldly yellow-orange light.

Top left: The skyline of Vancouver is not quite as famous as that of Manhattan, but in the light of the dawn sunshine it is no less beautiful.

Bottom left: The little town of Telegraph Cove on the north coast of Vancouver Island resembles a Norwegian fishing village.

Top right and below: Huge cruise ships glide along the coast of Vancouver Island.

The First Nations of the Northwest Coast

Long before the Europeans arrived in the coastal regions of the Inside Passage, this region was home to one of the most highly developed indigenous cultures of North America. The original region inhabited by the Indians of the Northwest Coast extended from the Chilkat River in Alaska down to northwest California in the south. The Tlingit, Haida and Tsimshian settled the mainland of southeast Alaska as far as the Douglas Channel in British Columbia as well as the patchwork of islands of southeast Alaska and the Queen Charlotte Islands in Canada. The Bellacoola, Bellabella, Kwakiutl and Nootka occupied the central seaside region, which included the coast of central British Columbia as far as northern Washington State. The main difference between the various groups was primarily their different languages; their lifestyle and cultures were very similar. They were expert fishermen, since their principal resource was the salmon. In contrast to many other indigenous peoples, the hunter-gatherers of the northwest coast lived in settled communities, travelling seasonally only between their permanent winter villages and the fishing camps by the rivers. Since the large schools of fish only appeared during the brief summer months they had to preserve the surplus for the winter by smoking or drying it. The First Nations of the northwest coast thus developed one of the most important cultures on the entire continent. This applied especially to their crafts, for which wood provided the most important raw material. They are famous for their boats, the bows of which were decorated with artistically carved figures and which were up to twenty meters (66 feet) long. The Haida in particular became master boat-builders. The

inhabitants of the Northwest Coast also built longhouses, in which several families lived, of wooden planks. To mark special occasions the famous totem poles, which can still be seen almost everywhere on the Northwest Coast, were erected in front of the houses. The artistic carvings depict the totem animals of the individual families. There are totem poles erected in honor of dead chieftains, funerary poles which stood by the graves of senior tribal members and chiefs, and posts which marked the

entrance to the houses or were used for support in the house construction. All the poles show mystic figures, mostly intertwined animal and human bodies, which represent important events from the lives of the families and the chieftain. Also famous are the Chilkat blankets of the Tlingit. They were woven of cedar raffia or mountain goat's wool and were dyed with colors made from moss, tree bark or copper. These blankets were among a man's most precious possessions.

Unlike most other hunter-gatherer societies, the first inhabitants of the Northwest Coast formed ranking societies with a number of classes in a set hierarchy. At the top were the leaders and their families, a position which was inherited. Nonetheless, the potential leader had to prove that he was worthy of the position he had inherited. At the famous potlatches, the wealth of the individual was put on display. The term "potlatch" means "to give". The initiator of a potlatch gave valuable items to the guests, often a rival family which would then be obliged to reciprocate with a potlatch of its own at a later date, in order not to lose face or status. Status and respect could be increased not only through the acquisition of wealth, but primarily by giving it away again. Generally each individual would attempt to outdo the other at the potlatch, which sometimes led to regular "potlatch fights" in which goods were not only given away, but were actually destroyed. The preparations for a big potlatch could take several years.

Everything changed when the first Europeans arrived on the Northwest Coast. Initially the First Peoples profited from trading with the white man. They exchanged otter and sealskins for iron tools with which they could design even more magnificent totem poles, as well as new goods which they soon learned to integrate into their lifestyle. The Tlingit in Alaska in particular turned out to be skilled trading partners. The tribal chiefs controlled the trade and became middlemen in a flourishing trade between the Europeans and the Athabasca Indians in the interior. The period between 1840 and 1867 can be seen as a sort of golden age, at least as regards the material culture of the Tlingit. Handicrafts made rapid progress and economic prosperity grew.

The decline came faster than expected, however. Europeans introduced illnesses like smallpox, which wiped out entire families during the years 1835–1839. Over a space of only three years almost ninety-six per cent of the Lower

Chinook people fell victim to the disease. Those who were not killed by disease were finished off by alcohol. In contrast to the strict laws imposed by the Russian colonial government, American trading ships gave alcohol to the Indians, who often died a miserable death as a result. The entire lifestyle of the indigenous population changed. Even the famous pot-latches contributed to their ruin, since they took on ever-larger dimensions and thus destroyed entire existences.

During the 1870s and 1890s the commercial fishing industry developed along the Northwest Coast. The claims of the First Nations to their fishing grounds, which went back over generations, were not recognized. The fishing industry fished the estuaries of the salmon-rich rivers mercilessly and reduced the salmon stocks so dramatically that the results can still be felt today. The "unfriendly takeover" of the entire country across the Alaskan as well as the Canadian section of the Inside Passage through the white immigrants forced the original inhabitants further into the background.

The sale of the former Russian colony of Alaska to the USA in 1867 had far-reaching consequences for the First Nations. In 1884 the USA passed the "Organic Act", which made provision for an education programme for the original inhabitants as well as regulating land rights. That meant, in fact, that they should be "civilized". Their children were to learn English; it was forbidden to teach them in the language of the Tlingit. The indigenous peoples were also guaranteed that they would be supported in their claims to the land which they were working at the time, but they were not allowed to acquire a legal right to the land.

When the boundaries of the Tongass National Forest were established in 1907, including all land which was not privately owned, the land claims of the Tlingit were restricted still further. In around 1900 the lifestyle of the indigenous peoples had largely been adapted to that of "white society".

Paid labour and commercial fishing replaced indigenous subsistence farming. Family groups left their little villages in large numbers and

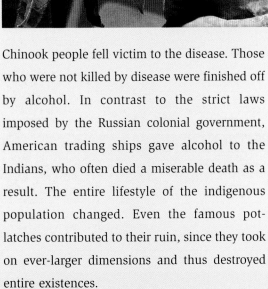

were much too small, the tribes could continue to hunt and fish and take part in publicly financed education and health programmes. In Canada, too, education meant primarily assimilation. On the other hand, the First Nations were denied Canadian citizenship. They were not allowed to own land, nor could they leave their reservations without permission. Even the Sun Dance and the potlatch were banned. White government agents had the right of veto on all decisions made by the tribal councils. It was also laid down by law who was actually an Indian. The Inuit in the far North and the descendants of mixed marriages were not covered by the Indian Act.

It was not until 1951 that the Indian Act was revised. The First Nations were once more permitted to leave their reservations without prior permission, and they were awarded voting rights, at least on a local level. During the 1980s and 1990s the individual groups were awarded greater rights of self-determination. But it is only recently that the Canadian government has promised the First Nations more land again, which has not been greeted with enthusiasm in all quarters.

In spite of numerous problems including unemployment and alcoholism, the future of the First Nations in general is no longer quite as negative as it was a few decades ago. The indigenous peoples are trying increasingly to come to terms with the overall situation. Tourism is expanding, which has a positive effect, at least as far as the economic position is concerned. Crafts are blossoming, and Indian guides take tourists to see the brown bears on the coast or arrange whale-watching tours. The timber industry values the assistance of the indigenous peoples when expanding into new regions. Even the great potlatch ceremonies are being held once more. It remains to be seen whether tradition and modernity can gradually form a symbiosis.

moved into the larger towns in search of work. The social structures broke down.

It was not until 1912 that the "Alaska Native Brotherhood" was formed with the aim of improving the life of the indigenous peoples and ending the discrimination in their everyday lives. They did not receive the right to vote until 1924, and only in 1946 did the Anti-Discrimination Act lay down their equal rights, at least on paper. The "Central Council of Tlingit and Haida" claimed a payment of US$ 80 million as compensation for the land which had been appropriated, but had to accept a much smaller sum in 1968. In 1971 they and other organizations representing the rights of the indigenous peoples of Alaska asserted their

rights in the "Alaska Native Claims Settlement Act": the indigenous peoples of Alaska were awarded almost 178,000 square kilometers (68,708 square miles) and the sum of almost US$ 1 billion. The indigenous peoples of southeast Alaska received some US$ 200 million. The "Sealaska Regional Corporation" took over the administration and fair distribution of the money. In return, the indigenous peoples agreed to renounce all further claims.

The development in Canada was similar: In the Indian Act of 1876 almost all aspects of the life of the First Nations was placed under government control. In return, the latter was obliged to protect the Indian reservations from seizure by white settlers. Within the reservations, which

From Seattle to Port Hardy
From Civilization into Wilderness

Every part of this earth is sacred to my people. Every shining pine needle, every sandy shore, every mist in the dark woods, every clearing an humming insect is holy in the memory and experience of my people. The sap which courses through the trees carries the memories of the red man.

Chief Seattl (1786–1866), chief of the Suquamish and Duwamish

Encounter with Killer Whales

The aircraft was slowly approaching the coast. The weather was magnificent. Seldom had I experienced such a clear day. The peaks of the Cascade and Olympic Mountains, snow-capped even in summer, were sparkling in the bright sunlight. The twin volcanoes, Mount Rainier and Mount Baker, the landmarks of the Seattle-Vancouver region, were at their most photogenic.

The plane started its approach and a short time later we touched down in Seattle – for many visitors "Mile 0" on the Inside Passage. We were 155 kilometers (97 miles) south of the Canadian border.

In 1851, a handful of settlers had landed at Alki Point and spent a harsh winter on the stormy coast. In the spring of 1852 they moved on to the more sheltered Elliott Bay – today's downtown Seattle.

The town itself was founded seventeen years later and named "Seattle" after the famous Squamish chieftain. The city's expansion began with the construction of the Transcontinental Railroad in the 1890s – a boom which has continued to this day. In 1962 Seattle hosted the World Exhibition, as a result of which many city landmarks such as the Space Needle, the Coliseum and the Pacific Science Center were built. Giants of the global economy like the software manufacturer Microsoft and the aircraft manufacturer Boeing have also established their headquarters here.

Today Seattle has almost 600,000 inhabitants, which makes it the largest city on the Inside Passage. It is also one of the most attractive metropolises in the whole of North America: its nickname, "The Emerald City", was chosen for a reason. When the sun shines (a rare occurrence), the city really does glow in an emerald-green light.

Seattle's location on the shores of the Puget Sound is spectacular, surrounded by a patchwork of small islands and fjords. To the west the city is framed by the snow-capped mountains of the Olympic peninsula and to the east by the ranges of the Cascade Mountains. Seattle was and remains a city built on the water. Puget Sound and a succession of small lakes shape the city's appearance and the lifestyle of its inhabitants. Even visitors anxious to press on should take time to view the city from above, from the observation platform of the Space Needle (185 meters/607 feet).

If you board one of the giant cruise liners which steam through the Inside Passage as far as Skagway, you will travel first along the Puget Sound, which extends over 145 kilometers (91 miles) from the Juan de Fuca Strait in the north as far as Olympia in the south.

Although the sound is a busy waterway, you will still have a chance of seeing dolphins and whales as well as huge freighters, tankers and fishing boats. The eastern coastal strip of the Puget Sound is one of the most densely populated regions in the entire northwest. With an area of 16,000 square kilometers (6,176 square miles) it is home to more than three million inhabitants.

To Vancouver

I decided against a cruise ship and traveled north towards the Canadian border along Highway 5 with a rented car instead. If you drive north from Seattle you will have the impression that you are traveling through one huge city. As far as Everett, one town gives way immediately to the next. I always endeavour to complete this section of the journey as fast as possible – I don't like the bustle here. After a

good 130 kilometers (81 miles) you arrive in Bellingham. This is where the ferries of the Alaska Marine Highway Systems embark on their voyage to Alaska. The next stop is Prince Rupert, the northernmost town on the Inside Passage which is on Canadian territory. However, if you want to explore beautiful Vancouver, pretty Victoria and the east coast of Vancouver Island you are advised to board the ship at a later point and to cross the Canadian border by car. Shortly after crossing the border

a small road branches off to Tsawwassen, the southern car ferry port for the crossing to Vancouver Island.

I continued a few kilometers further, however, since I wanted to visit Vancouver, which many regard as the most beautiful city in the world. The skyline is visible from afar. It would be a crime to ignore this city, which half the world adores. And so I headed for the canyons of the big city. Fortunately it was still early – the clock showed 6 a.m. The rush had not yet started and

everything was peaceful. Vancouver has some 580,000 inhabitants, which makes it about as big as Seattle and the third-largest city in Canada. More than two million people live today in the greater Vancouver metropolitan area. Simon Fraser is regarded as having been the first European to set foot in the region. He arrived here in 1808 on instructions from the North West Company. Twice there was a gold rush in Fraser Canyon and in the Cariboo Mountains, and during the 1860s thousands of people settled in the watershed of the Fraser River. The first permanent European settlement was established in 1862. In 1863 the first sawmill was commissioned, followed by others over the course of the next years. In 1867 a certain John Deighton settled on Burrard Inlet. "Gassy Jack", as he was called because of his big mouth, opened a saloon which he named "Gassy Jack's Saloon", around which a settlement soon grew – Gastown, the historic center of Vancouver. In 1870 the colonial government

renamed it Granville. The little village lay on a natural harbor and was therefore chosen in 1885 by the Canadian Pacific Railroad to serve as the western terminus of the transcontinental railroad. The town's expansion to a metropolis was sealed: the town itself was founded in 1886 and was named for the great explorer George Vancouver.

Today Vancouver is one of the cities with the highest quality of life in Canada. The great attraction it exerts on immigrants from all over the world is reflected in the city's ethnic composition. More than forty per cent of Vancouver's inhabitants belong to ethnic minorities.

Almost one third hails from China, making Vancouver's Chinatown one of the largest in the whole of North America, after those of San Francisco and New York. The Chinese settled here because of the gold deposits in Fraser Canyon and the construction of the transcontinental railroad.

Top left: The skyline of Seattle.

Bottom left: Spotlights illuminate the Parliament Building of Victoria, the capital of British Columbia.

Top right: You can enjoy the best view of Vancouver from one of the three nearby mountains: Grouse Mountain, Mount Seymour, and Mount Strachan.

Below right: Vancouver is booming. New buildings are going up everywhere; high-rise buildings are mushrooming.

Following double page: Sunset above Johnstone Strait in the north of Vancouver Island.

Despite its big-city character Vancouver has remained a very "green" city. Stanley Park, which measures 404 square kilometers (156 square miles), is the city's green lung and one of its citizens' best-loved excursion destinations. Vancouver is also famous for its delightful setting. To the north and east, the North Shore Mountains soar skywards. On fine days there is a magnificent view of the city and across the Strait of Georgia to Vancouver Island from the city's three closest peaks, Grouse Mountain (1231 m/4038 ft), Mount Seymour (1449 m/4753 ft) and Mount Strachan (1454 m/4769 ft). When it is exceptionally clear you can even see as far as the US state of Washington in the south. From here the snow-capped volcano Mount Baker looks like a giant from the Himalaya.

Unfortunately, days with good visibility are rare in Vancouver – to put it mildly. On average it rains here on more than 160 days per year. The climate is mild, but damp. The winters are among the warmest in the whole of Canada. The thermometer seldom sinks much below freezing point. The maritime climate means that the average winter temperatures here are nearly 2 to 4 degrees Celsius (4 - 8 °F) higher than farther inland. Vancouver is to host the Olympic Winter Games in 2010, and there are those who wonder how that will be possible given the city's mild, rather rainy climate. However, the alpine competitions will mostly be held in Whistler, some 130 kilometer (81 miles) away, a ski resort in the Whistler Mountains, which has fairly reliable snowfall.

If you are lucky with the weather, then a stroll through the historic city center is really to be recommended. Even I – a sceptic when it comes to big-city bustle – enjoyed walking through Gastown. The numerous cafés and attractive little shops are really worth a visit. And of course you should make a point of seeing the historic

steam clock, which hisses on the hour and regularly attracts a crowd of tourists.

After two days, however, I had had enough of the urban jungle, steam clocks and cafés. I had to get out into the countryside again. My next destination was Vancouver Island. The largest island of the North American continent is only a short ferry crossing away from Vancouver. So off I went, in search of whales, bears, rainforest and lonely beaches.

Vancouver Island

There are several ways of reaching Vancouver Island from Vancouver. North of Vancouver lies the little town of Horseshoe Bay. From here there is a ferry service to Nanaimo on Vancouver Island. Nanaimo, however, lay too far to the north for my purposes. And so I decided to head instead for Tsawwassen, which lies a short distance south of Vancouver. From here you can also take the ferry to Nanaimo. However, my plan was to head further south – to Victoria, the capital of British Columbia. And so I took the car ferry from Tsawwassen to Swartz Bay. The boats leave every hour, so it is not really necessary to make plans in advance. All the same, in summer Vancouver Island is a popular holiday destination for the citizens of Vancouver, who invade the island in hordes. Then the ferries are often very full, so that long waiting times are the norm. The earlier in the day you arrive, the emptier the ships will be. BC Ferries are like the ferries of the Alaska Marine Highway System. They are true freight ships but extremely comfortable all the same. The crossing to Swartz Bay takes one and a half hours. If the weather is good you will have a fine view of Vancouver and the volcano Mount Baker across the US border in Washington State.

Vancouver Island is about as large as the Netherlands, stretching more than 500 kilo-

meters (313 miles) from the island's southernmost point to its northern end. Vancouver Island boasts a total of 3340 kilometers (2150 miles) of coastline. In the south the Strait of

Left: Today the pretty wooden cottages built on stilts in Telegraph Cove mostly serve as holiday homes.
Below: Until a few decades ago, lighthouses were essential aids for ships as they navigated through the narrow straits. This is the Entrance Island Lighthouse. In the background, volcanic Mount Baker (3,285 meters/10,775 feet) rises into a cloudless sky.
Below and bottom rigtht: The coasts and beaches of Vancouver Island are a true holiday paradise. .

Georgia separates the island from the Canadian mainland; in the north, it is separated by the narrow Johnstone Strait and the Queen Charlotte Strait. In the far south the Juan de Fuca Strait lies between the island and Washington State. The mountains of the Vancouver Island Range rise to over 2000 meters (6560 feet), separating the wild West Coast which faces the Pacific from the more temperate East Coast. The climate is very mild; on the coasts in particular the temperatures seldom sink below freezing. In the mountainous interior, however, the winters are mostly damp and cold. On Vancouver Island you will still find largish continuous areas of temperate coastal rainforest, especially in the sparsely populated

northern half of the island and in protected areas such as the famous Pacific Rim National Park on the West Coast. Black bears, wolves, coyotes, and moose live here, but you will search in vain for a grizzly bear; the latter is only to be found nowadays on the mainland. The wolves have retreated to the far northwest of the island, to the Cape Scott Provincial Park. Vancouver Island can also claim the largest puma population in Canada. Few visitors are lucky enough to see this shy mammal. Twelve years previously I had been fortunate. As if in slow motion the majestic, but potentially dangerous, big cat ran across the road in front of me in the twilight. That was the last time I saw a puma in the wild.

Whales, dolphins, sea otters and seals, however, are less retiring. All these animals can be
seen in large numbers in the coastal waters. The
coast also offers a breathtakingly beautiful
underwater world, especially north of Campbell
River.

Today some 750,000 people live on the island,
most of them on the East Coast between

Victoria und Nanaimo – the coastal section
which forms part of the Inside Passage.

Victoria, the Capital

The mood of pleasurable anticipation increased
as the ferry terminal came into view. From
Swartz Bay I traveled by car along Highway 17

to Victoria. Those anxious to head for the
wilderness must be patient for a little longer.
During the past twelve years the population has
grown rapidly in this area and is now almost as
dense as on the mainland.

Like Vancouver, Victoria is without doubt one
of the most attractive towns in Western Canada,
compensating for any feeling that the wilder-

All images: Within the space of a just few days you can experience a wide range of moods in northern Vancouver Island: A bank of mist above Johnstone Strait (left), almost unreal-looking evening light above the Strait of Georgia (top right) and sunset near Telegraph Cove (bottom right).
Following Double page: Evening colours above Johnstone Strait.

ness is still some distance away. The town's origins go back to 1843, when the Hudson's Bay Company established a trading post here originally called Fort Camosun. It was later renamed Fort Victoria – in honour of Queen Victoria, who was Queen of the United Kingdom of Great Britain and Northern Ireland from 1837 until 1901. Victoria was incorporated as a city in

1862 and in 1868 it became the capital of the amalgamated provinces of British Columbia. For a long time Victoria was one of the busiest centers on the Northwest coast. In 1885, however, when the Transcontinental Railroad reached Vancouver on the mainland, the economic power and significance shifted to Vancouver instead. Nonetheless, Victoria

remained the political center of British Columbia. To this day, everything here is very British: the style of the architecture and the red double-decker buses which provide public transport. Victoria today has approximately 74,000 inhabitants; if you include the surroundings, the population total rises to four times that number. Among the main sights are the Parliament building, the famous Fairmont Empress Hotel and the entire Inner Harbor.

By chance I arrived in Victoria on July 1st, the Canadian national holiday. Canada Day commemorates the formation of Canada as a federal state within the British Commonwealth, as a result of the British North America Act on July 1st, 1867. On that day the city positively bursts at the seams and the atmosphere is highly contagious. Bands play beside the harbor, actors perform little plays and artists exhibit their paintings. Victoria is said to be the most popular retirement destination in Western Canada, but I have seldom seen so many young people in a town enjoying themselves in such a relaxed and pleasant mood as on this occasion in Victoria. Life here seemed somehow calmer and more relaxed than elsewhere. Maybe the climate also plays a part in that, because it is said to be the mildest in the whole of Canada. Victoria can also claim an above-average number of sunny days. It boasts on average no fewer than 2,183 hours of sunshine per year, and the rainfall is laughably low by Inside-Passage stan-

dards. With an average of 66.5 centimeters (26 inches) per year it has less precipitation than Vancouver and Seattle and also less that the famous Sunshine Coast on the mainland, to the north of Vancouver.

Northwards

After just one – fine and sunny – day in Victoria I set off again northwards along Highway Number One. From the road there are frequent fine views across the Strait of Georgia to the offshore Gulf Islands. Thanks to their convenient location between Vancouver Island and the mainland and their almost-Mediterranean climate, the Gulf Islands are a very popular excur-

Above: The receding tide has revealed a green carpet of seaweed. The tides along the west coast of North America should be treated with respect. Center and top right: Picture-perfect Inside-Passage weather. After pouring with rain all day, the sun emerges from behind the clouds for a few minutes during the evening and bathes the coast and the mountains in orange-colored light.

Highway 19 and took the 19A instead, a smaller road that offers a charming alternative to Highway 19. It runs almost the whole way along the coast, through countless small towns and villages. You will need a little time, however, because you can seldom drive faster than 70-80 kilometers per hour (44-50 mph) and the built-up areas run almost directly into each other. The seaside resorts are very crowded in summer, and are full of guest houses, hotels, motels, and holiday apartments. Little side roads lead off at regular intervals to relatively crowded beaches. I had to fight my way through crowded towns and heavy traffic as far as Qualicum Beach before I reached a beach which looked the way I thought a beach on Vancouver Island should really look. A fairly empty white-sand beach extended for miles with a magnificent view of the Coast Mountains on the mainland. That evening I went for a long walk on the beach and could feel that I was gradually calming down.

I stayed there overnight and drove early the next morning into the interior. A Canadian had given me the tip that a few miles from the coast, directly beside Highway 4, there was a region where Douglas firs grew which were up to 800 years old. Once upon a time, they had thrived throughout the entire island.

After less than half an hour I arrived at MacMillan Provincial Park, parked the car and headed on foot along a narrow path into the forest – into Cathedral Grove. These vast, ancient trees look like beings from another world as they soar heavenwards. They really do have the appearance of mighty wooden cathedrals. The largest have a diameter of up to nine (!!) meters (26 feet) and can be over seventy meters (230 feet) high. In earlier times, before the timber industry started to appropriate the coveted wood, these giant trees were widespread throughout Vancouver Island. Today they are

sion destination for the citizens of Vancouver and Victoria. Depending on the tides the archipelago includes more than 200 larger and smaller islands. Eight of the largest ones are on regular BC Ferries routes.

The south of Vancouver Island, however, can hardly claim to offer wilderness and lonely beaches. One town joins directly onto the next. At the height of summer these little resorts are overrun by tourists from Vancouver and nearby Seattle.

It took me half a day to drive as far as Nanaimo. With almost 70,000 inhabitants, Nanaimo is the second-largest town on Vancouver Island. Once again it was the Hudson's Bay Company which opened a trading post here in 1849 which subsequently grew into the town. The discovery of coal deposits marked the start of the town's expansion. Coal was mined here until the 1960s, but then supplies ran out. Today the town is almost exclusively devoted to tourism. BC Ferries arrive here several times a day from Tsawwassen and Horseshoe Bay, making Nanaimo the second-largest gateway to Vancouver Island. Here I turned off the main

Above: From the heart of Vancouver the seaplanes embark on their journey to their often-remote destinations along the coast or in the hinterland.

Top right: On a clear day you can see the famous volcano Mount Baker from Vancouver, although it lies in US territory.

Right below: Port McNeill is a picture-book Inside-Passage town: a little harbor, a handful of attractive restaurants, a main street.

Following double page: A school of dolphins accompanied us on our tour to the orcas of Johnstone Strait.

only found in large numbers in special conservation areas. I spent the entire day in the fairy-tale forest, revelling in the special atmosphere of the primeval woodland. That was just what I needed and what I had been looking for – a day surrounded by the unspoiled nature of Canada. Unfortunately even here there is a lot going on in summer. Both car parks are mostly full. If you are in search of peace and quiet you will have to head further into the forest.

I left the enchanted forest in the evening and continued northwards along Highway 19A. I spent the night in Comox and looked forward to

the following days as the surroundings became progressively wilder and more solitary.

In Little River, a few miles north of Comox, it is possible to take the ferry to Powell River on the mainland. Powell River lies on the famous Sunshine Coast, a coastal strip which enjoys an above-average number of sunny days. I decided, however, against the sunshine and in favor of fog, wilderness and peace. North of Black Creek lie Miracle Beach and Saratoga Beach, two really beautiful beaches, where travelers can rest and relax. There is a breathtaking view of the jagged peaks of the mountains on

the mainland. I pitched my tent on Miracle Beach and enjoyed the last rays of sunshine.

The next morning I continued to Campbell River. The town, with its population of some 30,000 inhabitants, is regarded as the Gateway to the North. It calls itself the "Salmon Capital of the World". For those wishing to travel further it provides what will be the last opportunity to go shopping for a long time. If you are traveling by boat, Campbell River marks the start of a picturesque and varied stretch which is not without its hazards. The Discovery Passage begins north of Campbell River – a stretch of the Inside Passage which is very dangerous because of its fierce currents. It links the Strait of Georgia in the south with the Johnstone Strait in the north. In the Seymour Narrows the current can reach a speed of up to 16 knots and the tides are also extreme. Even the captains of the largest and most modern ships are obliged to proceed with caution here. Over the centuries, many ships have been wrecked in these hazardous waters. They may be a nightmare for sailors, but for the local wildlife they are a paradise. Countless species of seabird, sea lions, seals, killer whales and migrating humpback whales can be seen here. Each year in late summer and fall, millions of salmon swim through the waters of the Discovery Passage on their way to their breeding grounds in the interior. That is the time when hordes of sports fishermen invade Campbell River.

In the Wilderness

Those traveling by car as I did will find that the solitude begins beyond Campbell River. The well-maintained modern Highway 19, which is

even a dual carriageway in some places, gives way to a small, winding country road. I had long ago left behind me the endless little towns and villages which I had found increasingly annoying in the south. The road led away from the coast into the interior – into the magnificent mountains of Vancouver Island: wild, untouched, lonely. Now, at last, I finally felt I was in the wilderness! If you look closely, however, you will see that nature here is not completely untouched either. The timber industry has been busy, so that entire mountain peaks have become the victims of clearcutting or complete forest clearance. It makes me really sad to see how entire areas of wilderness are destroyed overnight, as it were. And yet, in spite of these moments of sadness, I felt truly happy up here. After another 200 kilometers (125 miles) I returned to the coast and took the turning to Telegraph Cove, shortly before Port McNeill. It was a fortunate decision, as I was to discover over the next few days. Fifteen kilometers (9 miles) further on I reached the little township, although "township" is too grand a word. All it consists of is a handful of magnificent old wooden houses which stand on wooden piles above the sea and are linked to each other by a so-called boardwalk. Today the cottages are mostly rented out as comfortable holiday homes. The region is well-known for its large fish stocks and correspondingly you will find large numbers of fishermen here. Whale-Watching safaris in Johnstone Strait are also offered from Telegraph Cove. And those who wish to do so can also go on a day trip to see the mighty grizzly bears at Knight Inlet.

I decided to stay for a few days to explore the region. I pitched my tent on the rocky coast. Sitting in the tree directly above my head, watching me suspiciously, were two bald eagles. The next day it rained. The Coast Mountains on the mainland, which the day

before had glowed so beautifully at sunset in the fading light, were hidden behind the clouds. While drinking coffee in the little campsite restaurant I struck up a conversation with a Canadian. When he asked me if I fancied photographing bears, I was full of enthusiasm at once. Of course I fancied the idea! It transpired that the friendly elderly gentleman was the head of the "Bear viewing safari", which I had read about in a brochure. The excursion cost almost 240 Canadian dollars, but the chance of seeing bears was simply too good to miss.

We set off at 8 o'clock in the morning – across to Knight Inlet on the mainland. After a journey of over two hours the boat was gliding down the inlet. I was a bit nervous. I had been photographing bears for over ten years, but I still always found it an exciting experience to watch these majestic creatures. It was pouring with rain. How could I possibly expect to get a clear photo in such lighting conditions? We slowly approached the coast. Suddenly a grizzly, a magnificent specimen, emerged from the undergrowth. At first it was as if I was paralyzed. I was unable to take any photos but sat, mesmerized, gazing at the huge animal.

The brown bears in the coastal regions of Alaska and British Columbia are noticeably bigger than their inland cousins. Inland grizzlies very rarely have the chance to eat meat and are primarily vegetarians. The brown bears on the coast, by contrast, can eat their fill of fat, protein-rich salmon almost all summer long. The fish swim in their thousands up the rivers to spawn and then to die. The animal protein has a noticeable effect on the weight and size of the bears on the coast.

For almost five hours I sat in the pouring rain, photographing four different bears which were searching for mussels and crabs along the shore. It was still a bit early in the year for salmon. The bears' banquet does not begin in

British Columbia until the middle or end of August. It was June, and I made plans to return in two months to record the spectacle on film. After a nine-hour trip we returned to base.

The next morning it was still raining – typical for the north of the island. I knew it might be some time before the skies cleared again. I

Left: A thick pea-souper lies over Broughton Bay near Port McNeill. That is no reason for the fishing boats to stay in the harbor.

Bottom and right: In contrast to the densely-populated south, the north of Vancouver Island still offers wild, virtually untouched nature. Lonely stretches of coast, wild black bears, cheeky seagulls…

decided to explore the region more closely. On my way there I had noticed a place where at least twenty bald eagles were sitting perched in the trees. After driving for only fifteen minutes I had found the place again, but this time there were only two eagles – and they were too far away for a good photo. I would have to get closer.

I set off with tripod and photo equipment. Everything stank of fish! I was obviously standing on some sort of rubbish heap, where fish and wood chips from the nearby sawmill were disposed of. In spite of the "trespassers prosecuted" signs I marched on. When I reached the edge of the "rubbish tip" I could hardly believe my eyes. At least thirteen black bears were sit-

ting there, tucking into the discarded fish waste. Of course I immediately started to take photos, although I was definitely a bit nervous. I was only about fifteen meters (16 yards) from the bears. Oh well, I thought, I'm sure it will be all right.

After about half an hour I heard a furious voice shouting behind me: "Hey, what are you doing here? Are you crazy? Didn't you see the signs?" Alarmed, I turned round. It was one of the sawmill workers, who spent the next five minutes berating me. After his anger had dissipated somewhat he insisted on seeing the photos on my camera display. Suddenly he was full of enthusiasm and made me promise to send him a few photos by e-mail. That's Canada!!!

It rained almost non-stop for the next seven days. My initial enthusiasm gave way to frustration. And then, finally, the sun re-appeared. The weather forecast said something about "some sunny days".

I borrowed a kayak for the next three days and set out to explore the coast a little. Secretly I was hoping to see the famous killer whales, also known as orcas, in the Johnstone Strait. It was not my lucky day. I was not interested in joining a whale-watching tour because there are always too many tourists on board and the angle is not very favourable for photographing the whales. In the restaurant in Telegraph Cove I was given the decisive tip. The best whale watcher on Vancouver Island apparently lived in Port McNeill, a few miles to the north. I immediately set off for Port McNeill.

With the Orcas of Johnstone Strait

Port McNeill on Broughton Bay in the north of Vancouver Island is the sort of place I like. It has a little harbor, a main street, two largish supermarkets, a handful of small shops and two very nice cafés. People here live at their own pace, and life passes very calmly and peace-

Above: The coastal rainforest extends virtually as far as the sea. Only a narrow, usually rocky strip separates the trees from the water.

Top right: At low tide, a grey heron waits patiently for small creatures such as crabs and little fish.

Right below: Not shy, but nonetheless difficult to photograph: little stints are usually seen in groups and are constantly on the move.

fully. You cannot miss the shop belonging to "Mackay whale watching" directly beside the harbor. At first I was rather sceptical because I was quite determined not to join in one of the run-of-the-mill tourist trips to the whales. And so I decided on a sort of test run and bought myself a ticket for the next day. The next morning, of course, the weather was bad. I simply didn't want to spend the day surrounded by a

thick pea-souper with thirty other tourists, watching whales from a couple of kilometers away through a telescope.

It was not at all like that. In the speedboat were only ten other very nice Canadians, some of them even from nearby Campbell River. Captain Bill Mackay turned out to be a real expert on the coastal waters and he knew so much about whales that I quickly forgot all my reservations.

He had been offering whale-watching tours for the past twenty-five years. He was, in fact, the first person to take tourists in his boat to watch the whales. At the beginning it was only a handful of enthusiasts who went out with him. Today, in the high season, it could be as many as forty every day. Orcas, also known as killer whales or, less commonly, as blackfish, are members of the dolphin family and can grow to eight meters (26 feet) in length and nine tonnes in weight. These highly intelligent predators are to be found in both the northern and southern hemispheres.

The orcas of Johnstone Strait are some of the best-researched killer whales in the world. It was Michael Biggs who began to observe the whales in the north of Vancouver Island of during the 1970s and to investigate their characteristics. He spent years in these waters, and his research work is unique worldwide. Over the course of the years, with the help of many local assistants, he was able to photograph and identify each orca on the coast. He found out that there are two species of orcas on the coast of Vancouver Island: the "residents", which live along this section of coast permanently and which eat fish, and the "transients", migratory orcas, which mostly hunt seals and only visit these waters for a short period. He kept a careful record of all eighty-five "residents" and soon discovered that a number of groups lived off the coast. At the head of each group was always the mother. Her offspring remained at her side throughout their lives, even when they matured and started to breed themselves, and they traveled up and down the coast together. Not only the songs of the residents and transients differed from each other; each family also "spoke" its own dialect.

You will learn all that and much more on Captain Bill's tours. As long ago as the 1980s he supported Michael Biggs' research work as an

observer and reporter. He has an extremely fast boat which enables him to track down the creatures in the water very quickly. All the same, a whale-watching tour is no guarantee that you will actually see any whales, especially if your visit takes place too early in the year. During my first tour in June I was able to see a few orcas, but they were far too far away to be photographed. Nonetheless I didn't regret that first tour with the Mackays, not least because we were treated to quite different wildlife by way of compensation: Steller sea lions, seals, dolphins, bald eagles, black bears …

However, I didn't want to miss out on the orcas and so the next day I went out again. This time Tyson Mackay, the son of Captain Bill, was on board as our guide and explained to the "whale fans" what they wanted and needed to know. He is probably one of the best photographers of orcas in the world – I, at least was always amazed at his magnificent photos, which hang in the Mackays' office. And yet, the second tour was no better than the first as far as I was concerned. We saw some orcas, but they were far too far away to photograph. Tyson realized how disappointed I was and told me I must be patient. I was willing to be patient, but I was short of time. My ferry to Prince Rupert was due

Previous double page: The Sunshine Coast on the mainland across the water lives up to its name. The morning sun slowly appears above the mountains. A new day begins.

Facing page: If there are no orcas to see – which is rarely the case – Captain Bill Mackay will find some equally interesting wildlife: A seal eyes our boat sceptically (left). Steller sea lions enjoy the weak sunshine (top). A dolphin accompanies the boat, approaching to within a few meters (right).

Above: Heavy rain clouds hang above the east coast of Vancouver Island. The next few days it rained virtually non-stop.

Bottom: At the end of June you may spot the red foxglove along the roadside.

Right top and bellow: In MacMillan Provincial Park you can still admire the vast Douglas firs which are up to 800 years old and 70 meters (230 feet) high. They used to grow all over the island. Excessive clear-cutting has turned them into an endangered species.

to leave the next day. I promised the Mackays that I would return in six weeks to try my luck yet again.

Another Attempt

Exactly six weeks later I was back again. We were pleased to see each other once more. It was a beautiful day, with the sun shining in a cloudless sky. Half an hour later the first dolphins came up close to the boat; an entire school of them leapt out of the water. I took one photograph after another in a frenzy. A great

start! And then, finally, the first orcas. Imagine my surprise when they swam directly up to the boat. I was unable to clip a lens with a shorter focal length onto my camera sufficiently fast. Then they swam alongside the boat – close enough to touch – and leapt boisterously out of the water, soaking me. What a photo opportunity! But I hadn't expected the creatures to come so close to the boat and therefore had a telephoto lens on my camera. Almost panicking, I tried to change to a different focal length, but when I returned to the deck it was all over. If only I had been working with two different

cameras with two different lenses – as I often do! I was devastated. Once again, Tyson cheered me up and assured me that it had happened to him at least a dozen times. Tomorrow would be another day.

The next morning I was the first person to reach the harbor. Surely my lucky day would come – and, indeed it did. This time the whales did not leap out of the water directly beside the boat, but they were sufficiently close for me to be able to take a few good photos. I just enjoyed the next trip taking a few photos and relaxing as I watched the orcas swimming along the coast.

The "Blue Canoes" of the Alaska Marine Highway System

The "Blue Canoes", as the blue-painted ferries of the Alaska Marine Highway System are affectionately known by the locals, are the only ferries which travel the entire length of the Inside Passage from Seattle to Skagway. However, the ferries actually start a few miles north of Seattle, in Bellingham.

The ferry network of the Alaska Marine Highway System aims to provide a safe and reliable link to the outside world for the countless little villages and towns of Alaska, many of which are difficult to reach and frequently not connected to the road network. The ferry network is not restricted to the Inside Passage alone, but covers the entire southern part of Alaska including Kodiak Island. Since 1963, a total of thirty-two destinations in Alaska plus Bellingham (Washington) and Prince Rupert (British Columbia) are linked by ferry year round, in winter as well as in summer. There are currently eleven ships plying the routes. Some 400,000 passengers and 100,000 vehicles are transported annually.

In my view, the ferries of the Alaska Marine Highway are the best way of exploring the Inside Passage: they visit many small villages along the route which would otherwise only be accessible by (expensive) air travel. The "Blue Canoes" are actually freight ships on which you can easily take your car, a procedure which I warmly recommend all Inside Passage visitors to try. Even though roads are few and far between in the coastal region of the Inside Passage, especially in southeast Alaska, a car is nonetheless essential. Only by car can you explore the areas surrounding the little villages. What I like best about the ferries of the Alaska Marine Highway, however, is their unique flair. They have nothing in common with the frequently showy cruise ships; the atmosphere is friendly and casual – and the journey proceeds at a wonderfully slow pace. If you want to travel the entire length of the Inside Passage without a stopover, you can of course book one of the many cabins for the voyage, which will take several days. There is (fortunately) no entertainment program on board, but you will not suffer from boredom. The unique natural surroundings provide sufficient entertainment. Several times a day there are interesting information events led by the rangers of the Tongass National Forest, who have a base on every ship. They talk about the flora and fauna of the Inside Passage, local history, geology and of course the first inhabitants of the region. I have always

enjoyed voyages by boat. It is very relaxing and you can drink coffee or eat fish and chips in the attractive little restaurants.

Incidentally, I have never spent the night in one of the cabins, but have always spread my sleeping bag out on one of the many daybeds on deck and slept in the open air (under the heaters). The ships of this wonderful ferry network, which is as much a part of the Inside Passage as the rainforest and the calving glaciers, are probably the only place where you will find that.

The ferries do not visit the smaller places along the Inside Passage every day. It is therefore advisable to study the timetable carefully. The Canadian section of the Inside Passage between Prince Rupert in the north and Vancouver in the south is traversed by the US ferries without stopping. For example, on the route heading south, the boats do not stop until they reach Bellingham in the US state of Washington. The only Canadian port where the ferries of the Alaska Marine Highway System actually stop is Prince Rupert.

I recommend that you do not travel the Inside Passage by ship non-stop from Bellingham to Skagway (or vice-versa). You should allow at least two weeks in order to explore the little villages and their surroundings, and then take the next ferry a few days later. Of course you can combine the Canadian and US ferries, which may also prove worthwhile.

I can still remember the night I spent on the M/V Malaspina. The ship was just sailing across the Lynn Channel north of Juneau. It was a clear, starry night. I was lying on my daybed, warmly cocooned in my sleeping bag, when a loudspeaker announcement by the captain woke me at about 2 a.m. Still half-asleep, the only words I registered were "Northern Lights".

I was wide awake immediately. The entire heavens were moving; greenish-yellow lights danced above my head. I had seldom seen the Aurora borealis as clearly as that. After only fifteen minutes the spectacle was over. I looked around me: everyone was fast asleep.

Only an elderly man nodded knowingly at me, smiled and said three words which I can still remember clearly, twelve years later, as if it were yesterday: "Welcome to Alaska!"

The Great Bear Rainforest
From Port Hardy to Prince Rupert

Few people know the jungle, or care about it ... An organized tumult of growth, that's what those thick undergrowth woods are, and yet there is room for all. Every seed has sprung up, poked itself through the rich soil and felt its way into the openest space within reach, no crowding, taking its share, part of the "scheme." All its generations before it did the same. Mercy, they are vital! There is nothing to compare with the push of life.

Emily Carr (1871–1945 in B.C.), Hundreds and Thousands: The Journals of an Artist, January 1, 1936

In the Realm of the Spirit Bear

If you want to continue north from northern Vancouver Island, you will have to transfer to the ferry in Port Hardy, some fifty-five kilometers (34 miles) from Port McNeill. A boat leaves for Prince Rupert every other day. And if – like me – you want to travel to the very heart of the Inside Passage, you should reserve well in advance, because this section is particularly popular with Europeans, since it is regarded as the very epitome of the Inside Passage experience.

The ferry cast off from Port Hardy at 7.30 a.m. Between the northern end of Vancouver Island and Prince Rupert on the border between Canada and Alaska the ships sail through narrow sounds, along the Coast Mountains of the mainland on one side and myriad islands large and small on the other. When the weather is good the journey is sheer pleasure; the outside decks are fully occupied – no one wants to miss the grandiose natural spectacle. The boat makes its way through one of the most unspoiled landscapes left on Earth: the Great Bear Rainforest. The region received its name during the 1990s from various environmental groups which were concerned at the time about the survival of this delicate ecosystem.

The Great Bear Rainforest covers an area of 64,000 square kilometers (24,704 square miles) – twice the size of Belgium! The entire region is inaccessible by road – if you want to visit it, you must travel by boat. Like all rainforests in British Columbia, the Great Bear Rainforest is also a cool temperate rainforest. Three geo-graphical and climatic factors are necessary for its existence: sea, mountains, and high precipitation. Temperate coastal rainforests are found in North America, New Zealand, Tasmania, Chile, Argentina, and Japan. Almost sixty per cent of all the temperate rainforests on Earth have already been destroyed. The rainforests of North America once stretched from Alaska to California; today, fifty per cent of them have already been lost. The Great Bear Rainforest is one of the last great continuous regions of temperate coastal rainforest in the world. Estimates indicate that it is home to some 350 animal species, twenty-five types of tree and hundreds of species of fungi and plants.

From the ferry, of course, you can only see a fraction of this paradise, and yet the region appears to radiate an unreal air of enchantment. As it started raining, people made their way on deck and gazed in fascination at the coast. The wind conjured up ever-new cloud patterns and moods. Most travelers on this stretch of the coast of the Inside Passage were Europeans. The BC Ferries vessel takes almost fifteen hours non-stop for the stretch from Port Hardy to Prince Rupert. Those wishing to explore the region in more detail must transfer to a seaplane or travel in their own boat. Since 1996 BC Ferries also offers an alternative tour. The so-called "Discovery Coast Passage" takes two days and heads from Port Hardy to Bella Coola, a place on the mainland coast which is also accessible by road. The boat also stops en route at Shearwater, Klemtu and Ocean Falls.

After the ferry had left the harbor of Port Hardy in north Vancouver Island, it headed for the Queen Charlotte Strait. The coast of Vancouver Island provided protection, but after a short while the boat started to rock. It was passing through the Queen Charlotte Sound, one of the few places where the Inside Passage meets the open Pacific Ocean, thus exposing the unprotected ship to the storms of the open sea. Inexperienced passengers are not the only ones who can suffer from seasickness on this stretch of the route.

Left: In addition to the Alaska Marine Highway System, BC Ferries serve the Canadian section of the Inside Passage. If you want to sail from Port Hardy to Prince Rupert in summer you should make your reservation well in advance.
Bottom left: Unafraid of people: a bald eagle in the harbor at Prince Rupert.
Right below: Detail of a Haida totem pole on the Queen Charlotte Islands.

After about two hours the problems were over and we were back in calmer waters again. Now Calvert Island provided protection from the west. The boat continued along Fitzhugh Sound, a waterway linking Queen Charlotte Sound with Fisher Channel. From here it was roughly another 380 kilometers (238 miles) to Prince Rupert. In spite of the sheltered location between the mainland and the island the wind often blows quite strongly here. Late that morning we reached the small town of Bella Bella. The Hudson's Bay Company constructed Fort McLoughlin not far from the present settlement between 1833 and 1843. Over the years, increasing numbers of members of the Heiltsuk Nation settled around the station. The village grew – and Bella Bella was the result. Today some 1,400 inhabitants live here, mostly Heiltsuk. Bella Bella is, in fact, the largest town on the coast between Port Hardy and Prince Rupert. Not far from the town lies McLoughlin Bay, a port of call for BC Ferries which has been visited regularly since 1996 as part of the "Discovery Coast Passage" mentioned above.

Our ship glided slowly into Milbanke Sound and shortly afterwards reached Finlayson Channel. The channel is twenty-four nautical miles in length and marks the start of the so-called "Northern Canyons", a succession of long, narrow channels which extend from Milbanke Sound north of Bella Bella to Chatham Sound south of Prince Rupert. By far the most spectacular stretch of this section of the Inside Passage begins at this point. To left and right the mountains of Susan, Roderick,

Dowager and Swindle Island rise to heights of up to 800 meters (2624 feet). And on all sides: forest, forest, forest. I would have liked to leave the ship immediately in order to explore the coast more closely by kayak. By now we had reached the Princess Royal Channel, some sixty-one nautical miles in length and regarded as the very heart of the "Northern Canyon". Slowly, Princess Royal Island came into view. The captain had spotted a group of orcas. As if under magnetic attraction, all the passengers

rushed over to the right-hand side of the boat. For a moment I was almost afraid that it would capsize with so many people all standing on the same side to watch the whales.

I, however, stood on the left side because I wanted to see the coast of Princess Royal Island, the home of a very remarkable animal. This time it was not the orcas which I was seeking; I was very much hoping to see a Kermode bear. Perhaps I would be lucky – and one of my life's dreams would be fulfilled. I had been waiting fifteen years for this opportunity! The coast was magnificent; it looked wild and apparently untouched, with countless waterfalls crashing down. But there was no sign of a bear.

The Kermode bear is, in fact, a white black bear. The "Spirit Bear", as it is often called, only lives on a handful of islands within the Great Bear Rainforest. On the mainland there is also a small population near Terrace. The "white one" is not an albino, but rather a genetic sub-

Top left: The morning mist has settled above the Great Bear Rainforest. The rainforest between Port Hardy and Prince Rupert is one of the wildest, and least accessible regions along the entire Inside Passage. If you want to explore this region at close quarters you will have to travel by boat or seaplane.
Bottom left: A coastal brown bear searches the beach at low tide for shellfish and crabs.
Right above: The weather has turned. Not a single ray of sunshine will be seen on the Queen Charlotte Islands during the next few days.

species of the black bear. It carries a recessive gene which accounts for its white fur. The largest population of spirit bears lives on Princess Royal Island, where about every tenth black bear is white. Many of the dark black bears also carry the "white" gene but do not show it: if the creature only inherits the gene for white fur from one of its parents and from the other parent the gene for black fur, then the dominant "black" gene always triumphs. In order for a bear to have white fur it must inherit the "white" gene from both its parents. It is therefore possible for a black she-bear to give birth to two white cubs, while a white she-bear may give birth to two black ones.

For a long time scientists did not realize that many of the dark black bears also carried the genetic makeup of a spirit bear. Since only the white black bears were protected, many of the black bears which also bore the recessive gene were hunted and killed. Now they, too, are protected.

However, how can a hunter tell a black bear with a "white" gene from a "normal" black bear? That is a problem which no one has been able to answer so far. On Princess Royal Island at least, there is a total ban on bear hunting. The greatest danger for these rare bears today is the loss of their habitat through the felling of trees.

Since my early youth I had dreamed of encountering a spirit bear in the wilderness. If you want to actually see a bear in the wild you will have to leave the ship and take a local guide. You will also need plenty of patience, time and luck. I had reserved two weeks in September just for the spirit bear.

There are no permanently inhabited settlements left on Princess Royal Island today. Only a few signs remain to recall the glorious days of timber and fish processing. From on board ship you can see the canning factory at Butedale,

which is slowly falling to rack and ruin – a very depressing view.

After the ship had passed through the Princess Royal Channel, it headed for the next narrow waterway. That evening we reached Greenville Channel between Pitt Island and the mainland, which is 72 kilometers (45 miles) in length and marks the beginning of the final highlight along this section of the route. In some places the channel is only 300 meters (328 yards) wide and thus one of the narrowest points along the entire Inside Passage. Steep rocks and cliffs soar heavenwards to the left and right, punctuated from time to time by a magnificent waterfall.

Hardly anyone remained below deck. The passengers were standing by the railing, all gaping in amazement at the coast. Every now and then the ship passed through a bank of thick fog; occasionally the sun broke through the drifting clouds and a magnificent rainbow appeared in the sky. The water was almost as smooth as a mirror. It was an nearly otherworldy atmosphere.

That evening, at about 10.30 o'clock, we reached Prince Rupert, the end of our journey. The mood on the boat hovered between euphoria and sadness. Now we would have to return to civilization.

Previous double page: Thanks to their protein and calorie-rich diet of salmon in summer, the brown bears along the coast are much larger than their fellows in the interior.

Below: Dolphins love to surf in the bow wave of boats. They are constant companions on almost every boat trip.

Far right, top and below: The tidal pools are true treasure troves. Mussels, starfish and sea urchins shine in brilliant colours.

Prince Rupert and a Short Detour to the North

Boasting some 17,000 inhabitants, Prince Rupert is the largest town in the far northwest of British Columbia. For many of the small villages in the Great Bear Rainforest it is an important supply center. Although Prince Rupert is a relatively young town, the large stocks of salmon in the nearby Skeena River have attracted people to the region for centuries. Long before the white man appeared here, the Tsimshian fished for salmon in the river. During the 19th century fish factories and small vil-

lages sprang up near the river. The breakthrough, however, did not come until 1910, when the town was chosen as the terminus of the Grand Trunk railroad; in the same year, Prince Rupert was awarded its town charter. The most important source of income here is still fishing; every year, up to five million salmon swim upriver to spawn. The town is the site of the largest salmon processing factory in the world. Of course, here too, tourism plays an increasingly important role. Whale and bear-watching tours are offered at the little harbor, and you can also go rafting on the Skeena River. Prince Rupert is also the gateway to Alaska. If

81

you want to continue northward from here along the Inside Passage, you will have to transfer to the ferries of the Alaska Marine Highways System. The "Blue Canoes" of the AMHS put into the harbor here regularly – it is actually the only port on Canadian soil which US ferries serve.

If you have had enough of the sea, rain and fog, from Prince Rupert you can head into the inte-

rior of British Columbia along the Yellowhead Highway. Prince Rupert itself certainly gets its fair share of rain and dampness. An average of 236 centimeters (93 inches) of rain falls here every year – twice as much as in rainy Vancouver. The town is often justly described as the cloudiest in Canada: the skies are overcast for some 6000 hours every year. I have visited Prince Rupert on several occasions. Only on a

single occasion did I see blue sky, when the clouds cleared for a few hours one evening.

If you have a few days to spare and do not have to continue your journey immediately to Alaska or the Queen Charlotte Islands, I recommend that you make a detour to Steward/Hyder. This truly remarkable place lies about 500 kilometers (312 miles) along the Yellowhead Highway and from Kitwanga on the Steward-Cassiar

Above, left and right: At the end of the road, after a breakneck journey along a bumpy gravel track, you will finally reach the observation point overlooking the Salmon Glacier near Hyder. In spite of a flat tire and a few drops of sweat on the driver's brow, the journey is certainly worthwhile. The view of the mountains and the glacier tongue is simply magnificent.

Highway. Steward and Hyder are just a stone's throw away from each other and yet they are worlds apart. Steward is still on Canadian territory, but Hyder is already in Alaska. At the little border post the officials subject everyone entering the United States to close scrutiny. Once you have passed the border controls between Canada and the United States you are on Alaskan territory, but you will not get very far

because the road ends after a few kilometers. Never mind: for many visitors the really important thing seems to be the "trophy", the stamp in their passport to show that they have been to Alaska.

I first visited the place in 1997. In those days the ferries of the Alaska Marine Highway System visited the little place only a few times every month. Things have unfortunately changed

The place is regarded as one of the most easily accessible bear-observation places in the whole of North America. Anyone who comes here to see and photograph the bears fishing (black and brown bears) need not charter an expensive light aircraft as is unfortunately so often the case in the far north.

I visited the same spot again in 2006. It has become so famous that there is a real traffic jam on the car park in the evening, especially at weekends. A wooden boardwalk has been constructed to protect the viewers from the bears and Park Rangers are there to ensure the safety of the bear-watchers.

In spite of all the noise and bustle, the magic of the place has been retained. In August 2006 a

Previous double page: Because of the infinite variety of species living here the Queen Charlotte Islands are known as the Galapagos of Canada.

Above: The landscape recalls that of the Southwest United States: rock formations in the Tow Hill Ecological Reserve on Graham Island.

Below: The morning mist off the coast of Princess Royal Island is slow to clear.

Right: Visitors in search of peace, quiet and rest will find all they are looking for on the remote Queen Charlotte Islands.

now. When I arrived in Hyder in the evening ten years ago, I saw an entire train of cars driving along a gravel track which heads out of town for a short distance. Curious, I joined the queue. After a short drive we reached a car park overlooking a narrow river. A number of people were standing there and taking photos with huge lenses. I followed their gaze and could hardly believe my eyes. Several brown bears were standing there, fishing for salmon. I stayed for almost a week.

brown she-bear arrived punctually at the river at 7 p.m. with her three cubs and started fishing. The boardwalk was in danger of collapsing under the weight of the crowds. Nobody said a word; you could have heard a pin drop. An elderly lady from nearby Steward turned to me and whispered quietly: "That's great theater!" Probably she was right.

Once you have had enough of bear-watching, provided you have a reasonably robust off-road vehicle I recommend that you continue along the gravel track to Salmon Glacier. The track eventually runs directly alongside the glacier. Right at the end there is a magnificent view of the tongue of the glacier and the area which feeds it.

The Queen Charlotte Islands – Haida Gwaii

Back to Prince Rupert. I was standing in the supermarket, in the middle of a major shopping session. I was going to take the ferry to the Queen Charlotte Islands the next day and I didn't know whether I would be able to buy anything there. Strictly speaking the islands in the far northwest of Canada are no longer part of the Inside Passage region, but if you are in the area you should definitely make a detour to include them

In fact, the Queen Charlotte Islands would be worth a journey in their own right, because the archipelago is as beautiful as it is varied. If you

want to explore them properly you will need to allow plenty of time and should already have a certain amount of experience in wild places. It is best to join an organized boat trip. Most of them last several days, but it is only by boat or seaplane that you will really have the opportunity to explore the most remote bays, beaches and villages on the islands.

I had decided to explore at least the northern main island, Graham Island, alone and on foot and in my rented car. Car ferries leave Prince Rupert almost daily for the islands; the crossing takes about six hours.

Seeing the archipelago for the first time from a distance, I was immediately fascinated. *Haida Gwaii* is the name given by the famous Haida people to the island archipelago off the northwest coast of British Columbia. The two main islands Graham Island and Moresby Island form the heart of the island universe, along with more than 200 small offshore islands and islets. The flora and fauna here are so varied that the islands are often referred to as the "Galapagos of Canada". This archipelago is home to a great number of rare and indigenous species, that is, animals which only occur here and nowhere else. One of them is the largest sub-species of American black bears.

Some fifty per cent of the approx. 5000 inhabitants belong to the First Nations. Long before the Europeans set foot on the islands for the first time, the Haida had settled here. According to legend Haida Gwaii is the place where time began.

But time also evolved into the familiar drama. Europeans imported diseases which killed off a large percentage of the Indian population. Smallpox in particular annihilated entire villages. The European settlers seized the land and legal suppression did the rest. The highly developed culture of the Haida was at risk of slowly disappearing for ever. Today some 2000 Haida

Above: You will feel you have been transported into a fairy-tale world. Virtually every square centimeter of forest is covered with a thick layer of moss.

Right: A photo I had dreamed of taking for years: a bald eagle sitting on a thick, mossy branch in the middle of the rainforest.

Top right: At Fish Creek near Hyder you can observe the brown and black bears at close quarters from a safe observation platform.

Right below: Its time has come: in a few days this salmon will be dead. It has returned to the river where it hatched. Here it will spawn and die, completing the circle of life.

still live on the island. Fortunately there has also been a turn for the better. The Haida have started to think once more about their own culture; one visible sign of this fact is the Haida Heritage Center, which was opened in 2007. The Indian cultural center has been established in six typical Haida longhouses, in front of which stand six huge totem poles. The six poles represent six villages which in turn represent six clans. If you are interested in the history of the First Nations in the region you can join a guided tour through the museum and learn a great deal about it and the islands in general.

The museum lies not far from the place where the BC Ferries berth between Skidegate and Skidegate Landing.

The islands are virtually undeveloped; only on Graham Island is there a road which is 110 kilometees (69 miles) long and leads through the eastern part of the island. The ferries berth in Skidegate Landing. From here it is only a few kilometers to Queen Charlotte City, which has 1,200 inhabitants and is the second-largest "town" on the island after Masset in the north. Queen Charlotte City is an attractive little place with all the facilities one could wish for: a few

cafés, a supermarket, a gas station ...! The inhabitants live here – as elsewhere on the island – according to their own rhythm. Everything happens very slowly, at a leisurely pace. For me the little town was important primarily as a place for purchasing supplies, since I wanted to continue to the Naikoon Provincial Park in the northeast of Graham Island. On this trip I unfortunately had to omit a visit to the paradisiacal Gwaii Haanas National Park because of lack of time and for organizational reasons; if you can manage it, however, you should definitely spend a few days there,

although it is only accessible by chartering a seaplane or joining an organized boat tour.

In the language of the Haida, the name *Gwaii Haanas* means more or less "Islands full of wonder and beauty". The National Park consists of over 130 islands with a unique flora and fauna. It is famous for the tidal pools which form along the coast at low tide. The sea retreats by as much as eight meters (26 feet) leaving behind pools which serve as habitat for a wide variety of marine species. The creatures which have adapted to this environment have a hard struggle for survival. They have to cope with both wet and dry surroundings. These tidal pools often glow in the most beautiful colours. Starfish shine in bright shades of red, orange and purple. If you look closely you will also spot, in addition to the starfish, coral, sea anemones, shrimps, sea urchins, shells, sponges and sea snails. Although you can actually find similar tidal pools along the entire length of the coast of the Inside Passage, those in Gwaii Haanas National Park are among the most beautiful. The abandoned Indian village of Ninstints on Anthony Island can only be reached by boat or plane. In 1980 the village was listed as belonging to the World Cultural Heritage. It is famous for its weathered old long-houses and totem poles.

After stocking up with provisions in Queen Charlotte City, I drove past the Haida Heritage Center and the Ferry Terminal to Skidegate. With a population of some 700 inhabitants it is

regarded, together with Masset, as one of the twin cultural centers of the Haida. However, I was only passing through. The modern, tarmac road now leads along the picturesque east coast of the island to Tlell, a village with 370 inhabitants at the southern end of Naikoon Provincial Parks.

From here you can take one of the attractive hiking paths through the park, but I wanted to approach the park from the north instead. So I continued a bit further along the Yellowhead

Highway into the interior. Soon I had reached Port Clements on the east bank of Masset Inlet. Almost 600 inhabitants live here, mostly from fishing and forestry. From here the nearly straight road leads in a northerly direction. After driving for a total of two hours I reached Masset. The largest town on the island has a population of 1,500 and is considered an important center of Haida culture. In the historic village "Old Masset" you can admire the fine old totem poles.

Previous double page: It is rare for the sun to shine in a cloudless sky as here off the coast of Princess Royal Island.
Top left: A perfect picture: For a few precious moments the rising sun bathes the east coast of Graham Island in a dramatic light.
Right above (all images): In the Haida Heritage Center on Graham Island you can admire the famous Haida totem poles. The carvings show the family totems, mostly mythical figures, interwoven animal and human bodies.

Beyond Masset the road becomes more of an adventure. A gravel surface and deep potholes allow only slow progress. The countryside becomes wilder, and the route now continues along the north coast of Graham Island and leads further and further into Naikoon Provincial Park.

Naikoon Provincial Park extends over 73,000 hectares (180,310 acers) and is primarily famous for its long, lonely sandy beaches and for its almost untouched rainforest. The forest is really remarkable – an enchanted forest. Everything is covered in moss, and the trees soar heavenwards like extraterrestrial beings. Fallen tree trunks lie criss-crossed on the ground and look like trolls or gnomes from a fairy tale. I walked through the forest for two days taking photos. It was pouring with rain but I hardly felt a drop because the green canopy above me was so dense. The atmosphere was dark, almost threateningly so. After two days the sun came out and I decided to go for a walk along the beach. If you like wild and lonely sandy beaches which extend for miles, you will love the coastal strip of Naikoon Provincial Park. The surf here thunders on the shore. There are no offshore islands to protect the coast from the stormy Pacific Ocean. I hiked to one of the geological sights of the park, Tow Hill (109 meters/358 feet). The hill, made of basalt deposits, is one of the highest points in the park and was formed by volcanic activity some two million years ago. The rocky coast in the Tow Hill Ecological Reserve looks as if it was carved by human hand, with the rocks often lying parallel to each other. When the last rays of sunlight bathe the cliffs in a deep crimson you could almost imagine you were in the canyons of the southwest United States.

After about a week I had to leave the islands again – very reluctantly, I have to admit. I am sure I shall return one day.

In Search of the Spirit Bear

During the summer of 2006 I was traveling from Hyder (Alaska) along Highway 37a towards the Stewart-Cassiar Highway when, suddenly, a she-bear ran across the road in front of me with her two cubs. The bear was white. I could hardly believe my eyes – a Kermode bear, a white black bear up here on the mainland is a very unusual sight. For years I had read every book, every article about the white black bears, which all said that it was primarily Princess Royal Island and the surrounding region which were most famous as the habitat of these unusual bears. I immediately parked the car by the roadside and waited. The mother bear had retreated into the undergrowth with her two cubs – only three or four meters from the road. I could hear the twigs cracking, but the bears did not reappear. I waited by the roadside for over an hour, but in vain. I was on the verge of despair. But I made a decision. The following year I would devote an entire trip to the search for the Kermode bear.

On September 10, 2007 I stood at the little seaplane airport in Prince Rupert, waiting with four other passengers for the seaplane which would take us to Hartley Bay. That was to be the starting point for our tour into the realm of the spirit bears. Our guides, Eric, Trish and Nikki, were already waiting for us. Our group consisted of five "bear enthusiasts": my old friend Marcus, Clark and Carol from Alberta, Robina from Ontario, and myself. We all shared the same wish: to see the spirit bear and, of course, to photograph it. We clambered aboard the *Great Bear II*, a nice little boat with every comfort, in which we would spend the next seven days sailing through the waters surrounding Princess Royal Island. Eric, Trish and Nikki come from Vancouver. Eric and Trish are specialists when it comes to tours through the Great Bear

Rainforest – but the Spirit-Bear Tour is definitely their favourite. Nikki, Eric's niece, was basically there for fun and helped the others whenever she could. On the first evening Trish showed me the photos she had taken the previous week. I was almost lost for words at what I saw. The

All images: The Great Bear Rainforest is home to the rarest bear in the world: the white black bear, also known as the Kermode or Spirit Bear, is a genetic sub-species of the black bear. The Spirit Bear is only found on a few islands off the coast of British Columbia and at a few locations on the mainland.

Following double page: Dawn on a lonely beach on Graham Island.

pictures showed a black mother bear with her two white cubs.

At four o'clock that afternoon Eric started the engine and we set off. The weather was magnificent, with not a cloud in sight. Eric headed for Gribbell Island, a small neighboring island near Princess Royal Island; he explained to me that white black bears lived on the smaller islands surrounding Princess Royal and that the chances of encountering one there were very high because of the higher population density. We were slowly approaching the coast of Gribbell Island; Eric, Trish and Nikki scanned the beach through their binoculars. They knew from experience that the bears liked to come down onto the beach at low tide to search for

shellfish and crabs. The rest of us gazed in fascination at the beach. The earlier we saw a bear, the more relaxed the trip would be. I told Eric and Trish that I was working as a photographer on a book about the Inside Passage and that for me it would simply not be complete without the region's most important animal, the Kermode.

After we had been sailing for about two hours Trish shouted: "Over there, in the bushes! A white one!" We all stared in the direction in which she was pointing. And indeed, surrounded by green undergrowth, there stood a white black bear. To my sorrow it was too far away to photograph. But all the others were happy. After just five minutes the bear trotted back into the bush and disappeared.

95

Top left and opposite: The sky is mostly covered with clouds along the Inside Passage. And when the sun does manage to struggle through, a unique spectacle occurs.

Left below: The rock near Skidegate on Graham Island bears the appropriate name of "Balance Rock".

I was disappointed: no good photo of a white bear. Eric and Trish had already realized that I would be difficult to please. We continued along the coast and an hour later we saw the next spirit bear. He was strolling calmly along the rock. The evening light was wonderfully soft.

Slowly, slowly we sailed in closer until we were at a good distance for a photograph. I took one picture after another. The boat was tossing a bit, which made it quite difficult to get a sharp picture with a 600 mm lens. The bear was kind enough to wait another few minutes before dis-

appearing into the dense forest. But I had my spirit bear photos and was indescribably happy. That evening everyone was relaxed, but I was restless again. Now I wanted to get a photo of a bear in the rainforest, if possible with a salmon in its mouth.

The next morning we set off for Princess Royal Island. The weather was fine again, without a single cloud to darken the steel-blue sky. I, however, was not so happy about that because it is virtually impossible to photograph a bear well in the rainforest when the weather is fine:

the contrasts between light and shade are too harsh. On my many journeys I had often had bad weather and had been grateful for every ray of sunshine. Now, when I would have preferred not to have any sun, it was shining as if it would never stop!

The next three days we saw no more bears, neither on Princess Royal Island nor on Gribbell Island. We watched humpback whales, seals, bald eagles, but no Kermode bear. My spirits were at an all-time low. The sun was shining mercilessly – as it had done for the past four days. I had never experienced weather like it in the Great Bear Rainforest. All my hopes were now focused on the last two days. On these days Marvin, a guide who was a member of the Haida people, was to lead us along a salmon river in which white and black bears were accustomed to fish. We heard Marvin's boat very early in the morning. According to Eric, Marvin was one of the very best guides around, and could mostly be relied on. I took to Marvin at once; he was always friendly and always smiling. Early that morning he took us to the salmon river. The sky was almost cloudless. I thought to myself that there was no chance of success.

The first hours beside the river passed quietly. A number of black bears came to catch fish. Marcus was delighted and took one shot after another; it was his first bear trip. I, however, was only interested in the white bears. While we were waiting the black flies were busy; after a short time my hands were badly bitten and I could hardly bear the irritation. I was amazed at the equanimity with which my Canadian companions put up with this torture. Marvin told me a great deal about the white bears and their importance for his people – and also how the bears got their white color: "A long time ago, when the world and all the animals were still white and everywhere was covered in ice and snow, the Creator turned to the people and promised them a better place to live in. He turned the mountains which were covered in snow and ice into fertile land. But as a warning to Man that he should always appreciate these riches, he left every tenth bear white."

At about midday I was so tired that I could have fallen asleep on the spot, but the mosquitoes kept me awake. My eyes heavy with sleep, I gazed upriver – and saw a white black bear some distance away. I was wide awake at once. The bear came closer and closer and was eventually only ten meters (30,28 feet) away from us. The other group members were delighted. I, however, cursed quietly because the sunlight was too bright for me to be able to take good photos. I could scarcely disguise my disappointment. And yet, hope springs eternal …

The next few hours were spent waiting. The sun disappeared behind the mountains; the river lay in shadow. Now he could come, I thought to myself; now the light is perfect. Nothing happened. Eric was starting to insist that we should leave. Suddenly there was the sound of twigs breaking in the undergrowth downstream from where we were, and a magnificent spirit bear made his appearance. At last! He was ambling slowly towards us. I turned the ASA counter on my digital camera up to 800. The spirit bear came closer and closer. I became very calm and

kept taking photos. Then he strolled directly opposite us on the other bank of the river, stopped briefly and looked directly into the camera for a fraction of a second, directly into my eyes. I shall never forget how happy I felt in that moment.

Now, as I write, I can see the spirit bear before me as clearly as on that memorable day. Marvin was just as delighted as I was – not so much because of the bear, but because of *our* delight and *our* good fortune. He said that the more people took an interest in the Kermode bears, the better it would be for his people as well as for the bears. He really was a remarkable man. The next day we only got a brief glimpse of the Kermode bear, but no one was disappointed. That evening Trish cooked us an excellent supper and we all felt we were in seventh heaven. When we returned to Hartley Bay it was pouring with rain. It was hard to say goodbye to Eric, Trish and Nikki. I have seldom taken part in such a well-organized tour with such friendly, helpful guides. I shall return one day – the white black bear has worked its magic on me.

An Endangered Paradise

The problem starts on Vancouver Island. Entire mountaintops have been deforested. Ecosystems that took thousands of years to mature have simply been razed to the ground.

It was more than ten years ago that I first came across the wonderful book *The Great Bear Rainforest* by Ian and Karen McAllister, in which the authors drew attention to the threat to the rainforest posed by the timber industry. Suddenly, public attention was focused on the Great Bear Rainforest. In the 1990s a violent argument broke out between various environmental organizations on the one hand and the government and the timber industry on the other.

Time and time again, the environmental protectionists raised their voices in energetic protest. Major industrial concerns like the clothing manufacturer Patagonia discovered the spirit bears for themselves and stepped in on the side of the environmentalists. In 1999 Greenpeace organized a trip for German paper manufacturers and newspaper publishers to the forests of British Columbia, so that they could see the destruction for themselves. Thereupon the German trading partners threatened the Canadian paper industry that they would cancel contracts worth millions of dollars if the deforestation did not stop.

At last, in 2001, came the first success: the felling of old growth forests over an area of 1.2 million hectares (2.96 million acers) was stopped. It took another five years for the provincial government of British Columbia to place 1.8 million hectares (2.45 million acers) of primeval forest under a protection order on February 7, 2006. It now seems that untouched valleys such as the Koeye, Ahta and Aaltanhash valleys will be saved from deforestation. That is a positive result and can be seen as an important success, but it is hardly a reason to relax. Even in protected areas, hunters are still allowed to shoot "trophy animals" such as bears and wolves. Furthermore, no consideration was given to creating a continuous link between these protected areas. Roaming animals such as bears and wolves need at least a corridor joining the protected areas.

Furthermore the salmon, the most important link in the food chain of the Great Bear

Rainforest, upon which almost all life here depends, has only partly been included in the protective package.

The worst thing, however, is that only about thirty per cent of the entire region is protected thus far. Seventy per cent of the forest is still available for the timber industry as a source of raw material. An ecosystem which is unique in the entire world is still threatened in spite of this partial protection. Scientists estimate that at least forty-four per cent of the region would need to be protected in order to preserve the range of species (biodiversity) living there.

Travelers who have experienced the magnificent natural surroundings of the Great Bear Rainforest, who have felt and smelt the forest with all their senses; who have watched a majestic grizzly bear catching salmon and who have seen the spirit bears in their natural habitat will share my indignation that tree-felling and trophy hunting are allowed to threaten this wonder of nature. The government of British Columbia has promised that by 2009 ecological forestry will be introduced into those parts of the Great Bear Rainforest which are not yet under protection.

We can only hope that the government and the timber industry keep their word and that in future what remains of the forest will be treated with greater care than in the past.

From Prince Rupert to Sitka

Off to Alaska – the Last Frontier

To the lover of pure wilderness Alaska is one of the most wonderful countries in the world. No excursion that I know of may be made into any other American wilderness where so marvelous an abundance of noble, newborn scenery is so charmingly brought to view as on the trip through the Alexander Archipelago to Fort Wrangell and Sitka.

John Muir (1838–1914), Travels in Alaska II, 1879

Bears, bears and much more!

I was sitting in my car at the Prince Rupert ferry terminal waiting for the ferry. The Matanuska was to carry me across the first stage on Alaskan territory, as far as Ketchikan. Dozens of RVs were also waiting at the Ferry Terminal. A general mood of excitement prevailed because we were all heading for Alaska, the very epitome of wilderness and adventure! I, too, was full of anticipation. Not because the Canadian section of the Inside Passage was less beautiful and less exciting, but the very sound of the word "Alaska" sent a thrill of excitement down my back – even after fifteen trips.

Southeast Alaska or the *panhandle*, as the southern part of Alaska is known because it is shaped like a frying pan, is a remarkable region, even by Alaskan standards. While central Alaska, further north, is rightly known as "the ice-box of the United States", the climate in the southeast is much milder. On the other hand, here in this northern section of the Inside Passage, rain is still the determining factor. The countryside, too, is very different from that in the northern section of Alaska. Everything here is much more dense and closely-packed than in the north; the horizon is not so far away. Here you will find neither the treeless tundra nor the endless expanses of coniferous forest which characterize the taiga. As in Canada, temperate rainforest is the dominant vegetation in Alaska. But unlike the Canadian section of the Inside Passage, the landscape of southeast Alaska is characterized by mighty glaciers, which is no doubt one of the reasons why some people find the northern section of the Inside Passage more spectacular.

The Tongass National Forest, which covers 69,000 square kilometers (26,634 square miles), occupies over eighty per cent of the land area of south Alaska; it is the largest national forest in the United States. In 1907 US President Theodore Roosevelt placed the forests of southeast Alaska under state protection. Roosevelt admired the work of the famous scientist John Muir, who had carried out a scientific study of Glacier Bay in the north in the 1880s and 1890s, and wanted to support the work. It would be wrong, however, to imagine the Tongass National Forest as a continuous expanse of protected forest. To this day it is a forest which is used in a wide variety of ways; twenty-two per cent of its area, for example, can be used by the timber industry. Fortunately, however, there are also protected areas like the Misty Fjords National Monument and the Tracy Arm Fjord near Juneau.

If the Queen Charlotte Islands are regarded as the "Galapagos of Canada", then the panhandle can be justly described as the "Serengeti of the USA". More than 15,000 bald eagles and thousands of brown bears live here. Then there are the black bears, humpback whales, orcas, grey whales, dolphins, seals, sea otters, wolves, puffins, Arctic goats, marmots, elks, deer and wolverines. The region is the home of 75,000 inhabitants including large numbers of Tlingit, the people to whom the Tongass who gave their name to the forest also belong. There are also Haida and Tsimshian communities. Over half the population lives in Juneau, the capital of Alaska.

The road network is patchy. There are roads about twenty to thirty kilometers (13–19 miles) in length around the bigger towns such as Ketchikan, Juneau and Sitka; then even they peter out into nothing in the middle of nowhere. It is only in the far north that southeast Alaska is linked by road to the outside world. In Haines the Haines Highway links the region with the

Alaska Highway in the neighboring Yukon Territory, and the Klondike Highway leads from Skagway to Whitehorse, which is also in Canada in the Yukon Territory. Otherwise you are dependent on boats and seaplanes for transport.

The Inside Passage continues for some 500 kilometers (313 miles) through the Alexander Archipelago off the coast of Alaska, a chain of more than 1000 islands which stretch from Prince Rupert as far as Skagway. Especially in southeast Alaska the Inside Passage is less clearly defined than in Canada, since there are several channels which lead northwards through the labyrinth of islands. Many of the large cruise ships still berth at Ketchikan in the south; they mostly no longer make a detour to Sitka in the west but head instead on the fastest and safest route to Juneau. Along this section of the route I prefer to take the ferries of the Alaska Marine Highway System, since they travel several times a week between the count-

less smaller and larger towns along the panhandle. In the following account I shall therefore follow primarily the routes taken by the "Blue Canoes".

To Alaska

Having passed through the fairly complicated customs examination in Prince Rupert, I was pleased to be on board ship at last. I immediately reserved a recliner on deck, directly beneath one of the many heaters. At 6 p.m. the ferry cast off in Prince Rupert, glided out into the Chatham Sound and soon crossed the imaginary border between the United States and Canada. The next part of the journey was a relatively dull section of open sea. It is not until the ship reaches the Revillagigedo Channel that the landscape becomes more varied and therefore more interesting. In the west the ship passed Annette Island and then headed directly towards Ketchikan on Revillagigedo Island.

Alaska. In former times it was the site of a Tongass fishing camp. The first Europeans settled here during the 1880s, attracted by the large stocks of salmon. Until the 1980s, fishing, mining and logging were the most important industrial sectors in town. For the past thirty years, however, tourism has played an increasingly important role, since the big cruise lines decided to include Ketchikan as one of their ports of call. At the turn of the millennium the ocean-going giants brought more than half a million people to the town each year – and the upwards trend continues. The little town center has adapted to cope with the crowds of tourists. Many of the downtown shops only open when a cruise ship has docked in the harbor.

Today Ketchikan has about 7,500 inhabitants; tourism experts describe it as a town of superlatives. Ketchikan calls itself the "Salmon Capital of the World", the "Rainfall Capital of the World" and the town with the largest collection of totem poles in the world. It is also the centre

Top left: A bad-weather front has passed over Ketchikan and its surroundings. That evening the sun appeared and bathed the coast in a lovely warm light.
Bottom left: A shrimp trap near Petersburg.
Top right and below: Petersburg is known as "Little Norway", not only because the little wooden houses bear a strong resemblance to those in Norway. The man who founded the settlement, Peter Buschmann, was also a native of Norway. Today fishing is the main source of income.

of Indian culture in Alaska and famous as a "Sport Fishing Capital".

I have no problems believing that Ketchikan is the "Rainfall Capital of the World". It was pouring when I arrived. On previous visits, too, I have always only experienced Ketchikan in the rain. Each year an average of up to 400 centimeters (157 inches) of rain per square meter (1.2 square yards) falls here. At first sight the town centre, which consists of brightly colored wooden houses, looks very attractive. Unfortunately one quickly realizes that many of the little shops sell nothing but tourist souvenirs. It is much more interesting to stroll through the former red-light district in Creek Street. Until the 1970s prostitution flourished here. Today a wooden walkway leads along a little brook running through the district, and instead of the brothels you will find still more souvenir shops for tourists.

If you have a car at your disposal you should definitely make a trip to the Saxman Totem Pole Park, where a large number of magnificently carved totem poles made by the Tlingit people are on display. You can even see the artists at work in their studios in the park.

What I found most interesting in Ketchikan was the large number of bald eagles sitting around all over the place. Like the pigeons at home, here you will see in the early morning an eagle sitting on virtually every roof. It is really quite an experience to be able to observe these majestic birds at close quarters.

Ketchikan is the gateway to one of the most unspoiled wilderness regions in North America: the Misty Fjords National Monument. Bordered by the long arms of two fjords with steep granite cliffs and waterfalls which are a hundred meters (328 feet) high, some 3,600 square kilometers (1390 square miles) of total wilderness await the visitor. There are no footpaths and the visitor is thrown back on his own resources.

Those who wish to experience this wonder of nature are recommended to join an organized tour with an experienced guide. Days of continuous rainfall can be off-putting, but those who are prepared to put up with the rain and who have the right equipment will be able to experience a wilderness that is totally untouched by humans.

After four days of continuous rain with just one hour of sunshine, however, I was pleased to leave Alaska's "First City" again, and to board a ship of the Alaska Marine Highway once more. The next port of call was Wrangell.

Shortly after leaving Ketchikan the ship reached Clarence Strait. In the west you can see the coast of Prince of Wales Island, after Hawaii and Kodiak Island the third-largest island in the United States. Although most of the island is covered by state-owned forest, the logging industry has been very busy here. Bare mountaintops bear sad witness to its operations.

The ship reached the little port of Wrangell late that morning. It was pouring with rain when I disembarked for a week's photography at one of the best bear observation points in the world. I had just two hours to buy provisions. Wrangell is the only town in Alaska which has been ruled by four different nations during the course of its history: the Tlingit, Russia, the United Kingdom and the United States. Today, its 2,500 inhabitants lead quiet, stress-free lives. The main sources of income, as in most of southeast Alaska, are fishing and logging, although tourism is becoming increasingly important too. Wrangell is the gateway to the Stikine River and the Le Conte Glacier, the southernmost glacier in Alaska which calves into the sea. The Stikine River in particular, one of the three largest and most important river systems of the entire Inside Passage, has always been very important for the inhabitants of the region. The Tlingit used to travel inland along the river, most of

which runs through the territory of British Columbia, in order to trade goods with the Tahltan (also known as the Nahanni). From 1838 onwards, the Hudson's Bay Company also used the 640 kilometer-long (400-mile-long) Stikine as a transport route, establishing a number of trading posts along its banks. Today the

Previous double page: A black bear proudly displaying his prey? No – the hesitant look is directed at another bear which has set his sights on the salmon.

Top left: What a magnificent, powerful-looking creature! A black bear chases a salmon.

Bottom: The rainforest at Anan Creek looks virtually impenetrable.

Right below: Anan Creek is full of salmon. It is almost impossible to see the riverbed.

Right far below: The bald eagles have also set their sights on the salmon.

river is a paradise for rafting enthusiasts: the rapid current (740 cubic meters/962 cubic yards per second) makes it one of the best rafting rivers in the world. Sports anglers will also find what they're looking for, as the river delta is a popular salmon spawning ground.

However, I had only one destination in mind in Wrangell: Anan Creek, which lay some two hours by boat south of town in the middle of the rainforest.

The Bears of Anan Creek

When I visited Anan Creek for the first time in 1997, I thought I must be dreaming. In the very heart of the rainforest, several black bears stood fishing for salmon in an unprepossessing-looking stream. In the trees surrounding the river sat numerous bald eagles. The small stream was so full of salmon that you could hardly see the

riverbed. On that occasion I spent five days there – a paradise for photographers – and came to the conclusion that I would definitely return some day.

And here I was again. Back in January I had booked the little cabin directly on the shores of Anan Bay, the only accommodation in the vicinity of Anan Creek. Camping is not permitted here – it would be too dangerous because of all the bears. We set off at noon. Eric, my guide, who had brought me to Anan Creek eleven years previously, grinned as he asked me if I had enough film with me this time. I replied: "No, but I do have enough memory cards and batteries." How times change. The journey to the cabin took about two hours. I was a bit excited. Had I remembered everything? Had I enough food for a week? Where were my second and third cameras …? After two hours I could see the cabin in the distance; virtually

117

nothing had changed. Eric helped me to unload my luggage and then left. I had a slightly uneasy feeling as I stood there alone.

The furnishings in the hut are spartan, but nonetheless comfortable. I put away my luggage and set off immediately for the stream. A little wooden walkway leads through the rainforest. Progress was slow. I kept on stopping to fix my camera onto the tripod so I could take photos: of the rainforest in every imaginable variation; of the tree trunks and the branches – all overgrown with moss, creating bizarre shapes. After somewhat more than half an hour I reached Anan Lagoon, where the stream flows into the sea. At the lagoon I was met by a Ranger from the Wrangell Rangers District. Over the years Anan Creek has become popular as a bear observation spot, to such an extent that the Rangers have had to step in to regulate the flow of visitors. Each day only a handful of groups are permitted to watch for bears. They have to announce their visits long in advance. The Ranger checks the permits and tells the visitors the main rules of how to behave if you

Above: Late evening on one of the ferries of the Alaska Marine Highway System. A gap in the clouds opened up and provided us with this sunset. Right: In the middle of Sitka, five bald eagles sit on a tree as they watch out for something to eat. Following double page: From Harbor Mountain near Sitka you have a fantastic view. On the far left you can make out Mount Edgecumbe.

encounter a bear, which can happen on your way to the rapids or indeed anywhere in the forest. It is important above all not to frighten the animals, no easy task in the rainforest, because you mostly don't see them until they are standing in front of you. I showed my seven-day permit and told the Ranger that I would be living in the Anan Bay Cabin for the next week. He

was a little concerned because I was on my own and warned me to be careful, especially when walking through the dense rainforest. On the twenty-minute walk to the observation platform I felt absolutely safe. I repeatedly came across black bears, but they disappeared at once as soon as they sensed I was approaching. Black bears are by no means as aggressive as grizzlies,

119

which is why I was so relaxed. I finally reached the observation platform – a wooden "fortress" built into the rock. From here I had a very good view of the river. Another Ranger was standing on the platform, since it often happens that a bear tries to take over the "fortress". It consists of two floors: from the top one you can watch the bears and below, in the so-called hide, you can sit, well-camouflaged, and take photos of the bears at eye level. The hide was built into the rock down below, almost on a level with the stream. It is covered with camouflage netting and has only small spy holes to look out of. I clambered down and waited. Less than half an hour later the first black bear appeared. The river was full of leaping salmon, but the water level was high because of the amount of rain which had fallen, so that it was not at all easy for the bear to catch a fish. However, he seemed to be an expert. He snapped at the water and emerged with a salmon wriggling in his mouth. A good start, I thought to myself, and waited attentively. Nothing happened. After another hour I clambered back up. The next days would be better, the Ranger assured me. Fortunately I had planned to stay for a week.

That evening I tried to make myself comfortable in the little hut, but I ended up crawling to bed early and fell asleep immediately. At 1 a.m. I woke with a start; there was a scrabbling noise which seemed to come from the veranda. I cautiously opened the door: a New World porcupine was attacking my tripod, which I had left lying outside. I politely asked him to leave and he retreated at once. At 3 a.m. I heard the scrabbling again. Somewhat annoyed, I threw open the door with the intention of frightening off the porcupine more effectively this time – and found myself looking straight at two frightened young grizzlies. They fled immediately. Although it was dark I could see them running along the bank of the stream with their mother. Wow, that could have been dangerous. All the same, I was pleased about their visit. A family of grizzlies on the veranda of my cabin –

Above: A greater yellowlegs searching for little animals in the tide pools.

Right: A walk along the beach at low tide is always worthwhile. The receding tide has revealed some particularly fine sea urchins.

Top right: Once again, the clouds almost brush the surface of the sea.

growth at exactly 8 a.m. every morning and the mother fished for salmon directly beside my hide. The two cubs waited impatiently on the river bank for their meal. I had never seen anything like it in my fifteen years of traveling to Alaska. I had seldom seen such an attentive and careful mother bear as this one. Moreover, she was by far the best salmon fisher in the whole of Anan Creek – the male bears could have learned a thing or two from her.

I spent one day photographing the bald eagles in the moss-covered trees. Anan Creek is one of the few places where you can take such good pictures of the eagles.

All too soon it was time to leave. I had filled sixty gigabyte of storage cards, a record for a week's photography. I was sad to leave the place again. I had spent a week among the bears and had never felt as safe as I did there. As a result of my last years of traveling in Alaska I had stopped believing in the myth about the aggressiveness of bears. My experiences at Anan Creek had modified my opinion yet again. Of course the bear is a predator, but it is not a creature one need fear at all times. Bears are shy, magnificent creatures which can only survive today if we humans treat nature with respect.

I said goodbye to the friendly Rangers who had accompanied me through the ups and downs of bear photography for a whole week, and then I waited for Eric in front of the log cabin. I heard his boat while it was still far off. We nodded to each other in greeting. During the journey to Wrangell I didn't say a word – and nor did Eric. I think he knew how I was feeling.

Further Northward

That same day I took the ferry Le Conte from Wrangell to Petersburg. I had happy memories of Petersburg. Some ten years previously I had

nobody would believe me; that's Alaska, that's the wilderness. The next morning I told the rangers about my nocturnal visitors. It seemed the bear family was well known. They told me to keep my eyes open and store all my food in the food locker.

The next day the water level was not quite so high. I spent almost the entire day in the hide taking photographs as if there was no tomorrow. Fortunately there were not too many day trippers. The journey to this magical place was clearly still too tiring for most of them. More and more black bears, and even brown bears, came to the river. As soon as a brown bear appeared, the black bears were gone in a flash: the two species are deadly enemies. There are not many places in the world where you can watch both brown and black bears fishing for salmon in the same stretch of river. Anan Creek is one of these remarkable places.

During the next few days I was able to take all the photos I wanted: various black bears which demonstrated remarkable skills as they caught the salmon, and a number of brown bears. The highlight was a black she-bear with two tiny cubs. The family emerged from the under-

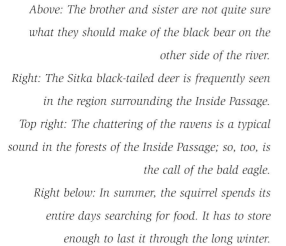

Above: The brother and sister are not quite sure what they should make of the black bear on the other side of the river.

Right: The Sitka black-tailed deer is frequently seen in the region surrounding the Inside Passage.

Top right: The chattering of the ravens is a typical sound in the forests of the Inside Passage; so, too, is the call of the bald eagle.

Right below: In summer, the squirrel spends its entire days searching for food. It has to store enough to last it through the long winter.

124

spent almost a week there in brilliant sunshine. Even the journey to Petersburg, through the Wrangell Narrows, was an experience. The big cruise ships avoid that stretch of water: it is too narrow, with too many shallows, and therefore too dangerous. That is the advantage of the Alaska Marine Highway ships. They are relatively small and nimble and are therefore ideally equipped for these dangerous waters.

Petersburg, at the northern end of the Wrangell Narrows on Mitkof Island, is a picture-book Inside-Passage village. The brightly colored wooden houses are very attractive and recall those of Norway. That is not surprising as it was Peter Buschmann, an American of Norwegian extraction, who built a fish factory and a sawmill here in 1897. He was followed by many of his "Norwegian friends", and thus a "Little Norway" developed in the heart of Alaska.

Today some 3,200 people live in Petersburg. The most important source of income by far is fishing. The village is home to the biggest halibut fleet in the entire country. The summer months are high season. Workers from all over the world come to work in Petersburg, in order to process over 50,000 tonnes of fish.

The income from tourism is also becoming increasingly important. Petersburg is not one of the ports of call of the big cruise ships because the harbor is too shallow for their draught, but the little town's charming location has made it famous. Increasing numbers of tourists use Petersburg as an ideal starting point for their trips. From here you can easily reach the nearby Le Conte glacier. It is also an ideal starting point for a boat trip into Frederick Sound, where you can get a grandstand view of humpback whales. Humpback whales come to the waters of Alaska during the summer months in

order to eat their fill of krill (tiny shrimp) and herring. They spend the winters in tropical waters, for example off the coast of Hawaii.

For me, the town of Petersburg is primarily a fine place to relax, to follow a few picturesque trails through the rainforest, to watch the fishermen as they go about their work and to walk along Sandy Beach near the town. After four days I left Petersburg. I wanted to press on to Kake, a tiny settlement on nearby Kupreanof Island.

Kake – Another Bear Paradise

The boat glided into Frederick Sound. Most of the passengers were staring at the sea. They all wanted to see the humpback whales for which the 160-kilometer-long (100 mile) sound is famous. Unfortunately none of the gentle giants appeared. My disappointment was muted, however, because I knew I would not be able to take any good photos from such a big ship and was

also aware that better opportunities awaited me further north. Some five hours later, Kake came into view. The Alaska Marine Highway ferries berth there twice a week. When I checked in for the voyage in Petersburg, one of the employees of the ferry system asked me in surprise what I wanted to do in Kake. I didn't know myself – I just wanted to visit the place. Gazing at the handful of houses I found myself wondering whether it was really the right decision to spend a few days here. Apart from me, only one single

passenger left the ship here. The village has some 800 inhabitants, most of them members of the Tlingit tribe. The village claims to possess the world's largest totem pole cut from a single piece of wood. And indeed it does rise heavenwards into the grey skies above the village, thirty-two meters (105 feet) in height.

It was raining, as was so often the case. The rain on the Inside Passage is different from elsewhere in the world. I always have the impression that someone "up there" must have turned

Previous double page: Every morning at precisely eight o'clock this black she-bear appeared on the shores of Anan Creek, to catch salmon for herself and her cubs. After a leisurely breakfast the entire family trotted happily away.

Top left: The sun slowly sets over Sitka Sound

Bottom left: For seagulls, too, the salmon is an important source of food in summer.

Right above: Marking the end of the day: yet another brilliant display of color above the fjords.

on the lawn sprinkler. The rain is so fine that it only takes a few minutes before you are soaked to the skin. I drove through the village and was on the point of driving back onto the ferry again when, in the little stream flowing through the village, I saw two black bears fishing for salmon. I immediately pulled in and trecked down to the river bed. Then I saw that there were not just two bears fishing, but four – no, five! In the middle of the village, five adult black bears were standing and fishing. I spent the next four days photographing bears from morning to night. I stood right in the middle of them, less than ten meters (33 feet) away. No bear, no human, was bothered. In a conservation area I would have been sent away immediately because there are good reasons why you should not get too close to a bear. But the bears of Kake remained peaceful and tolerated me in their immediate vicinity. They were probably used to being surrounded by people. A bear chased a salmon; there was a splashing in the water. He seemed not to have noticed me. I took one picture after another. Just a few meters away from me he stopped, a huge salmon gripped firmly between his teeth. For a fraction of a second he looked at me in surprise before slowly moving off. On the other bank he stopped to enjoy his catch. I immediately examined the pictures on my display – proof that I hadn't been dreaming. A bear with a salmon in his mouth was looking at me. Satisfied, I headed for the only restaurant in the village and treated myself to a large hamburger.

To Sitka – the Historic Capital

Early that afternoon I set off for Sitka, the former capital of Alaska. The *Taku* glided out into Frederick Sound and set course for Baranof Island and Chatham Strait. Strictly speaking,

Sitka, which lies in the far west, does not really belong to the Inside Passage. Nonetheless, the ferries of the Alaska Marine Highway System call there regularly. They berth at Sitka once a week when traveling in both a northerly and southerly direction. And then there are also a number of routes which just travel the stretch between Sitka and Juneau. What is more, the former capital of Alaska is so beautifully located that it would be unforgivable not to call in there.

Chatham Strait is the biggest waterway in the southeast. It is 200 kilometers (125 miles) long and up to 600 meters (1969 feet) deep in places and extends from the Gulf of Alaska in the south to the Icy Strait in the north. About halfway down the ferries of the Alaska Marine Highway System squeeze through narrow Peril Strait, which separates the islands of Baranof and Chichagof from each other. This section is yet another challenge for the captain and a delight for the passengers. The ship has to pass so close to the coast that it is possible to search for wildlife along the shore without binoculars. For mile after mile the boat glides past rainforest which looks virtually untouched. The trees grow right down to the water's edge. Countless bald eagles can be seen. With a little luck you will also see black bears, especially at low tide, when they search the beach for mussels and crabs.

If you arrive in Sitka from the south in one of the ferries of the Alaska Marine Highway System, you will berth during the early morning hours. In the height of summer, however, it gets dark so late and light again so early that only a relatively short stretch of the journey is in total darkness. It was my third visit to Sitka. I like both the town and its surroundings. Sitka's volcano can be seen from the ship: Mount Edgecumbe looks rather like the famous Mount Fuji in Japan. Its snow-capped cone rises 1000

Left: These two young bear cubs are still able to play on the beach without a care in the world. In a year's time their mother will leave them to fend for themselves.

Below: Three of the most important animal species along the Inside Passage in a single picture: bald eagle (top), raven (centre) and brown bear (below)

Right below: A fat salmon writhes in the bear's mouth.

Bottom right: The two young black bears must have been about six months old. I had seldom seen such an attentive mother as this female bear at Anan Creek.

Following double page: The Indian River Falls lie at the end of the six-mile-long Indian River Trail near Sitka.

meters (3280 feet) into the mostly cloudy sky. You can book a guided tour of the mountain in Sitka.

The town itself, with almost 9000 inhabitants, has had a lively history. Long before the European turned up, the Tlingit had settled in this strategically favourable location.

Everything changed in 1799. That was the year when the Alexander Baranov, a Russian employed by the Russian-American Society, landed on the coast where Sitka now lies. He was looking for new sea otter hunting grounds, as the fur trade was the main reason why "white men" chose to come to Alaska at that time. From the outset, the Tlingit were sceptical about the new arrivals. When Baranov left

again in 1800, tensions grew between the original inhabitants and the new settlers. In 1802 the Tlingit destroyed the new settlement and killed most of its inhabitants. Baranov returned in 1804 with a Russian gunboat and tried to persuade the original inhabitants to agree to a permanent white settlement. The Tlingit were adamant in their refusal – after all, they had lived on this spot long before the white man arrived. Baranov then gave orders to fire on the Tlingit settlement. The Tlingit who survived fled into the nearby forests.

Once again the colonial powers were victorious, and Baranov built a white settlement which was chosen as the capital of Russian Alaska four years later, in 1808. The little town prospered

131

and was soon nicknamed "The Paris of the Pacific". The inhabitants of Sitka must have got a shock on October 18, 1867: Tsar Alexander II of Russia sold Alaska, which was worthless to him, to the United States for 7.2 million dollars. Suddenly, over night, the citizens of Sitka found themselves living in a foreign country.

Sitka's Russian roots can still be found everywhere today. Built in 1844, the Russian Orthodox church of St. Michael is one of the landmarks. In the meantime, Sitka has also made peace with the original inhabitants. In Sitka National Historic Park the visitor can admire a collection of fine totem poles.

There are only two minor roads leading for a few miles out of town. Nonetheless it is worth traveling by car. The ferry terminal lies at the end of one of the roads, so visitors without a car will have to take a taxi or bus – not a problem, however, since there are plenty of both at the terminal.

If you are traveling by car, I recommend a detour to Harbor Mountain. A short way out of town there is a small, potholed gravel road leading up the mountain. The view from the top is breathtaking. To the south, Mount Edgecumbe soars skywards, and in front lie numerous

Above: Ketchikan is known as the rain capital of Alaska. An average of up to 400 centimeters (15 inches) of rain per square meter fall here every year. If the weather is friendly, a visit to Creek Street in the former red-light district is a must.

Top right and right below: A huge cruise liner has anchored in the harbor of Ketchikan. The town is a popular stopover for cruise ships. Crowds of tourists besiege the town in summer.

islands large and small. If you have no car you can also climb the mountain on foot; the footpath begins directly in Sitka.

It is also worth taking time to visit the Alaska Raptor Rehabilitation Center, which also lies a short way out of town. Injured birds of prey of all kinds are brought here from all over Alaska and are then cared for until they recover. Some, however, are too badly injured for a full recovery. They remain at the station, where they are cared for.

There are interesting daily tours during which, for example, you can observe a bald eagle at close quarters. The highlight is the release of a falcon which has recovered from its injuries. A crowd of local inhabitants gathers, together with tourists in summer. A selected person is permitted to release the bird.

Above: The rainforests of southeast Alaska look virtually impenetrable in places.

Below: Sitka has only a handful of offshore islands, so the surf crashes virtually unimpeded on the coast.

Top right: Many visitors to Southeast Alaska can think of nothing but bears, eagles and whales. But the region is also home to countless small bird species. There is even a humming bird living here.

Following double page: A sailboat is leaving the harbour of Sitka at sunset.

136

The waters around Sitka are also a popular place for sea otters. At the end of the 19th century the cute creatures were almost hunted to extinction as a result of the booming fur trade. Today a large number of them are fortunately to be found once more along the coasts of southeast Alaska. Several companies offer tours to the otters.

With a bit of luck you will also see humpback whales during your trip, since they have chosen the region around Sitka as one of their preferred hunting grounds. There is an abundance of krill and herring.

If you have a bit more time, you should also include a walk along the beach at low tide away from town. The receding tide reveals a large number of tidewater pools in which there are beautifully colored starfish. And those who want to see the rainforest at close quarters will also find that Sitka offers ideal opportunities. Thus a scenic footpath begins just a few kilometers outside of town: the Indian River Trail, which is about nine kilometers (6 miles) long, leads to a waterfall by the same name, the Indian River Fall. Walking along the path I almost had the impression I was in the tropics.

Everything is green and covered with a thick layer of moss, and it drips with water on all sides. The forest is so dense that the sun's rays hardly penetrate as far as the ground. The waterfall which gushes down the rock face at the end of the path could also be in the Amazon region. Few hikers come as far as this. You should make some noise as you walk, however, since the region around the Indian River is a popular habitat of bears.

After a week in Sitka and surroundings I stood at the ferry terminal once more, waiting for the ferry.

From Sitka to Juneau
The Capital of Alaska

And here, too, one learns that the world, though made, is yet being made; that this is still the morning of creation; that mountains long conceived are now being born, channels traced for coming rivers, basins hollowed for lakes; that moraine soil is being ground and outspread for coming plants, is being stored away in darkness and builded particle on particle, cementing and crystallizing, to make the mountains and valleys and plains of other predestined landscapes, to be followed by still others in endless rhythm and beauty.

John Muir (1838–1914), Travels in Alasca V, 1879

Glaciers, Fjords and Whales

At 3 a.m. the call to cast off was given. The *Taku* left the harbor and headed for Juneau, the capital of Alaska. I was looking forward to the town and its surroundings. The road network extends further here than elsewhere and the infrastructure is better, although you can still describe the region as wilderness. As on the outward journey, the ship once more navigated the narrow Peril Strait. It was night again and so unfortunately the coast could only be seen as a vague silhouette. The next morning the Taku reached Chatham Strait. The weather was magnificent; the sun was shining in a cloudless sky. Such days are a rarity in Alaska. It was 8 a.m. and I sat on deck on one of the many deckchairs, enjoying the warm sunshine. During the past five weeks it had rained almost all the time. The first signs of movement could be seen in the numerous tents which had been pitched on deck. The ship was slowly beginning to wake up.

The *Taku* glided along the coast of Admiralty Island. I had been here once before, ten years previously – on the other side of the island, in Pack Creek. With an area of almost 4,300 square kilometers (1660 square miles), Admiralty Island is the third-largest island in southeast Alaska and, more importantly, the home of 1,660 grizzlies. Admiralty Island is thus the island with more brown bears per square mile than anywhere else on Earth. The Tlingit call the island *Kootznoowoo* – "Bears' Fortress". Angoon, on the west side, is the only town on the entire island. In summer, Pack Creek is a favourite haunt of brown bears, which fish for salmon there. From a safe observation platform you can watch them as they attempt to catch the fish. On that occasion I got a seaplane to bring me to the stream. Unfortunately it rained so hard all day that I was unable to take any decent photos. Even so it was an experience to watch the mighty creatures catching fish. Anyone wishing to observe the bears at Pack Creek will need a permit which can be obtained easily enough on payment of a small fee at the Juneau Ranger District Office. In Juneau there are a number of companies offering transportation to the river by seaplane.

Juneau and Surroundings

On its way to Juneau the *Taku* traveled through the Icy Strait. This extends some sixty kilometers (38 miles) from Cross Sound in the Gulf of Alaska in the west to Chatham Strait in the southeast. To the north of the waterway rise the snow and ice-covered summits of Glacier Bay. From time to time smaller icebergs from calving glaciers drift into the waterway. In summer, Icy Strait is the best place to watch humpback whales apart from Frederick Sound near Petersburg.

It was early afternoon when the *Taku* reached its destination. The mighty Mendenhall Glacier, Juneau's most prominent landmark, is visible in the distance. At 3 p.m. the ship berthed in Auke Bay. As in Sitka, Juneau's ferry terminal lies some distance out of town. The big cruise ships, on the other hand, berth directly in Juneau itself. From the harbor it is only a short distance into the center of town.

Juneau lies on the Gastineau Channel and is framed by the snow-capped Coast Mountains. With a population of almost 30,000 inhabitants it is the third-largest town in Alaska after Anchorage and Fairbanks, as well as being the state capital. If you want to visit Juneau you will have to arrive by boat or plane: the town is

Previous double page: One of southeast Alaska's postcard motifs: Fireweed in full bloom. In the background you can see the Mendenhall Glacier, Juneau's nearest glacier.

Left: In Glacier Bay National Park the sun only shines on an average of three days per month. The mountains are mostly enveloped in thick cloud. On the beach of Bartlett Cove at the edge of the park I enjoyed the magical lighting effects as I thought with pleasurable anticipation of the adventure of Glacier Bay.

Bottom left and below: Impressions of the northern rainforest.

the only capital of a US state which is not linked to the highway network.

Juneau's origins stretch back as far as 1880. On October 3, 1880 Joseph Juneau and his partner Dick Harris found gold in a stream near today's city. They staked their claim and called the little settlement Harrisburg. News of the discovery of gold soon drew hordes of adventurers to the region. Within a year, the population had grown to three hundred. In a referendum in 1881 the citizens decided to rename Harrisburg Juneau –

much to the annoyance of Dick Harris, who accused his former partner Joe Juneau of "buying votes".

In 1900, Juneau became the capital of Alaska; from time to time discussions are held as to whether Anchorage, which is much larger, should become the capital instead. So far, however, the high cost of moving the administration has resulted in the idea being abandoned. More than half the citizens of Juneau are currently employed by the state. The second-largest

143

source of income is tourism. During the summer months, as many as four giant cruise liners may berth simultaneously in the harbor. Then the number of people in town doubles instantly. Like Ketchikan, downtown Juneau is heavily geared towards tourism. I have seldom seen so many shops selling souvenirs and kitsch as in Juneau city center.

Nonetheless, it does have a charm of its own. The brightly colored old houses, countless steps and the town's hillside location are reminiscent of San Francisco. Built in 1894, the Russian Orthodox St. Nicholas Church recalls the fact that Juneau, too, has Russian roots. The little church, painted in blue and white, can easily be reached on foot from downtown. Visitors who look forward to a pub visit after their long sea voyage will enjoy the "Red Dog Saloon". Although the pub caters very much to tourists and virtually all the patrons are foreigners, it is still worth a visit for the quaint interior decorations and the live music.

When I arrived the weather was glorious, and I decided to travel into Juneau as quickly as possible. I wanted to take the cable car to the top of Mount Roberts, the mountain overlooking the town. Somewhat reluctantly, I abandoned the Mendenhall Glacier and traveled into town as fast as possible. There was a huge crowd waiting at the cable car station; a cruise ship had just berthed. Fortunately there is also a footpath leading up to the summit. It was still quite early and the sun was not due to set until

10 p.m. I parked my car at the start of the footpath and set off. After about ten minutes I heard a rustling sound in the undergrowth. Then I saw a black bear by the roadside, feasting on some berries which he had found. This really is the only place where you might expect to see such a sight. I was only 500 meters (0.3 miles) from town. I made some noise and the bear headed off. The rest of the climb was without incident (sadly, I have to say); I met neither bears nor people. The latter all took the cable

Top left: When the clouds descend right down to the surface of the water and everything is a uniform grey, the bright red fireweed provides a striking contrast.

Bottom left: Seals relaxing on a light buoy.

Top right: From this perspective the stems of the cotton grass look like creatures from another planet.

Right above: On Mount Roberts, the mountain overlooking Juneau, you can observe the ice-grey marmots at close quarters.

car to the top. After walking for one and a half hours I reached the cable-car station at the top. Even from here there was a magnificent view of Juneau, the Gastineau Channel, Douglas Island and the surrounding Coast Mountains. After resting for a few minutes I continued to climb towards the summit. With a height of 1,119 meters (3670 feet) Mount Roberts is not exactly a giant, but it is the 1,119 additional meters of height which you have to ascend; the mountain really does start at sea level. The nearer the summit you come, the lovelier the view – and the fewer people there are out and about. Once I got to the top I took my first long break. I had the summit to myself. I lay down on the grass and fell asleep immediately. After a short while I woke up suddenly: there was something there. I looked around me. Another black bear? And then I saw what had woken me: a pale grey marmot, which was trying to get at my picnic.

The sun was slowly sinking toward the horizon; the light turned yellow, then orange... I took photographs until it was too dark. At 10 p.m. I looked at my watch. Damn! I had missed the last cable car. Fortunately I had a headlamp. Two and a half hours later I reached my car, dog-tired, and drove the twenty kilometers (13 miles) to Mendenhall camp site. I pitched my tent and crawled inside. It was a clear night. Tomorrow promised to be a fine day.

Mendenhall Valley

The next morning my alarm clock went off at 6 a.m. It was bitterly cold. The camp site lies directly beside Mendenhall Lake, an expanse of water fed by the glacier of the same name. The cold air of the glacier was very noticeable here. I struggled out of my tent. The sky was cloudless. I packed up my photo equipment and headed for Mendenhall Lake. The surface of the water was as flat as a mirror, with a light mist

floating above it. The entire tongue of the glacier was reflected in the lake. Half an hour later, the morning sun slowly appeared behind the mountains. The mist, the ice, everything gradually turned orange. I hardly knew what to photograph first: the glacier, the ice floes floating in the water, the mountains ... Directly beside me, no more than fifteen meters (49 feet) away, stood a beaver, gnawing at a branch.

An hour later it was all over. Now the sun was too high in the sky to take really beautiful pictures; ripples appeared on the surface of the water; and the beaver had returned to its dam. I sat on the lakeshore, ate my picnic and gazed at the vast glacier as it slowly made its way from the mountains into the valley.

John Muir, the most famous naturalist to visit Alaska, described Mendenhall Glacier as one of the loveliest in the entire state. In 1879 he named it "Auk" (Auke) after the old Tlingit settlement. In 1892, however, it was renamed Mendenhall Glacier in honour of Thomas Corwin Mendenhall, the superintendent of the US Coast and Geodetic Survey. Today it is the most easily accessible glacier in the southeast.

Mendenhall Glacier was formed during the so-called Little Ice Age some three thousand years ago, when the temperatures sank continuously and many of the mighty ice rivers in Alaska were formed. Until 1750 the glacier continued to advance, but since then it has retreated gradually. In those days the glacier tongue was more than four kilometers (2.5 miles) longer than it is today. Today the stream of ice and snow creeps forward by sixty centimeters (24 inches); unfortunately, the melt every day is slightly greater than this modest advance, with the result that the glacier is retreating. The current rate of loss is between seven and ten meters (23-33 feet) per year. Since the climate continues to warm up, it will not be possible to prevent the continued melting of the glacier. The mighty

Mendenhall Glacier is twenty kilometers (13 miles) long and is fed by the Juneau Icefield. The latter extends over an area of 2,400 square kilometers (926 square miles) and is the source of many glaciers in the region. Apart from the

Previous double page: The seaplane is one of the most important means of transportation in south-east Alaska. Many places can only be reached by boat or by air – including Juneau, the capital of Alaska.

Left: Downtown Juneau: the town has spruced itself up in anticipation of the arrival of the hordes of cruise tourists. In the background you can make out the cable car leading up Mount Roberts.

Below: The harbor of Auke Bay lies a few kilometers north of Juneau. The ferries of the Alaska Marine Highway System dock here.

Far right: The Russian Orthodox Church of St. Nicholas is one of the top ten sights in Juneau.

Mendenhall Glacier, the Juneau Icefield also feeds the Lemon Creek, Herbert, Eagle and Taku glaciers with snow and ice.

The Mendenhall Glacier Visitors Center was opened in 1962. It lies directly on the shores of Mendenhall Lake and affords a magnificent view of the lake and the tongue of the glacier. Here you will learn all you need to know about glaciers. Films about the glacier, Mendenhall Valley and the flora and fauna of the glacier regions are shown in a small lecture theatre. A few meters away you can take your photos of the glacier from the so-called *Photo Point*. Unfortunately it is often very crowded there, especially when the passengers from the cruise ships arrive at the glacier in coaches. There are better, lonelier, places where you can admire the glacier. In spite of the bustle, however, it is worth visiting the Photo Point, not so much for the view of the glacier but rather because of the

many Arctic terns, the coastal sea swallows which nest here and glide above your head. I had often tried to photograph these fascinating but aggressive birds, but had never been able to get close enough. As soon as I approached the birds would start to dive down at me in defence of their nests. But at Photo Point the birds had clearly realized that the crowds of people meant no harm, and allowed me to take my photos without problems.

Mendenhall Valley is not only a favourite haunt of the Arctic terns; you will also find black bears and bald eagles here. Arctic goats graze high up in the mountains on the green meadows, and large shoals of salmon swim upstream up the Mendenhall River. You can watch them in the smaller tributaries of the river in the late summer and early fall. Until recently the valley was also the home of a black wolf. The inhabitants had grown quite fond of "their" wolf, until

it was shot by someone whose identity remains a mystery until this day. The locals were furious and even offered a sizable reward for the person who discovered who had killed the creature.

If you want to enjoy the glaciers in peace and quiet, I recommend that you stay at the campsite beside Mendenhall Lake. From the lake-shore you have a magnificent view of the mighty tongue of the glacier. If you want to get even closer and are prepared for a mountain hike, you should walk along the path which skirts the northern side of glacier tongue. The path is often very muddy after heavy rain and is then very tiring to walk along, but it leads directly along beside the tongue of the glacier and into the region from which the glacier is fed. Time and again you will have a magnificent view of the dark blue, shimmering ice. With a bit of luck you can also spot the timid Arctic goats whose preferred habitat is high up in the mountains.

If you are not quite fit enough for that, you can hire a helicopter at Juneau Airport to take you on a flight over the glacier – including, of course, landing on the ice.

All images: Southeast Alaska is a land of many moods. It is mostly during the first and last minutes of the day that such exquisite plays of light can be observed. (Top left) The sun breaks through the clouds above Lynn Channel. (Top right) Sunset over Lynn Channel. (Right below) Morning dawns at Mendenhall Lake.

Those who prefer to travel by raft, kayak, or canoe, will find ideal conditions in Mendenhall Valley. A number of firms offer rafting tours on the Mendenhall River and kayak and canoe trips on Mendenhall Lake.

It is a wonderful experience – but potentially a dangerous one – to paddle your kayak up close to the huge icebergs which float on the lake.

If you decide to approach the place where the glacier flows into the lake by kayak, you should be very careful because the glacier calves without any proper warning. It is not only the blocks of ice which pose a danger as they crash down; there is also a huge flood wave which rolls across the lake when larger icebergs break off.

Whale Watching with Captain Harv

In Auke Bay, the little harbor a short distance north of Mendenhall Valley, I went searching for someone who offered whale watching tours. Of course there are plenty of whale watchers here, but their boats were all too large for my purpose and were designed to carry too many passengers. I was looking for a small boat with space for not more than three or four passengers, so that I would be able to photograph the whales at eye level. Quite by chance I overheard a conversation about whales in the port. I only heard snatches of conversation, like "bubble feeding" and "breaching" and was immediately all ears. I joined the group and discovered that the man wearing the baseball cap was called Captain Harv and that he had been offering trips to see whales for many years. He showed me his boat – small, easy to manoeuvre and big enough for a maximum of five passengers – just what I was looking for. I hired his boat for the evening hours.

We set off at 5 p.m. Just two more photographers joined me on board. We traveled north from Auke Bay for about half an hour; Captain Harv had last seen a group of whales there that morning. Indeed: the whales were still there. From afar we could see their water fountains glittering against the light. The whales were among the four hundred-odd members of their species which swim every summer up the fjords of southeast Alaska, attracted by the large stocks of fish and krill. Humpback whales need to eat about a tonne of food every day in order to build up sufficient reserves of fat to survive the winter. During the winter months they play in the warm waters off Hawaii and Mexico, where they mate and give birth to their young. During this period they do not eat at all.

Captain Harv was delighted: "They are still bubble feeding." Everyone on board knew what that meant. "Bubble feeding" is a special hunting technique employed by humpback whales.

Previous double page: Diamonds of ice: floating ice floes from the Mendenhall Glacier in the lake of the same name.

Above: The dark clouds look almost threatening. Within a few hours the weather has changed completely.

Right: A huge block of ice floating in Mendenhall Lake sparkles in the light of the rising sun.

Top right: Mendenhall Glacier at close quarters. You should always exercise caution when approaching these huge ice structures as they can turn and break without warning.

We had now reached exactly the spot where we had seen the whales a bit earlier. All was quiet. Suddenly, the captain called out: "Over there, they're just surfacing." And indeed, an entire group of humpback whales suddenly emerged from the water, their mouths wide open. It all happened so quickly that I didn't manage to get a single photo. My consolation was that my two colleagues fared no better.

Captain Harv explained to us that you never know where the whales will appear next. We should watch the seagulls instead. The seagulls can see from above where the school of herring is rising to the surface, and then they start to fly in circles. So I watched the seagulls. They were gliding back and forth, apparently aimlessly. The seagulls gathered in the air, just fifty meters (368 feet) from our boat. And then I saw the air bubbles on the surface of the water. I immediately set up my lens. All of a sudden, eight humpback whales sprang out of the water with their mouths wide open. I pressed the shutter release, only stopping when the whales dove back into the depths once more. The magnificent spectacle only lasted for a few seconds.

I immediately took a look at the pictures on by camera display. If only I had not done so! In that very moment a huge humpback whale leapt out of the water, just a few meters from our boat.

The technical term for that is "breaching". To this day, experts are uncertain why the whales do this. Some scientists think that it is no more than a gesture of joie-de-vivre on the part of the huge sea creatures.

My pleasure in life, however, had just been somewhat reduced. I was not able to take a picture of the leaping whale!

During the course of the evening we saw at least ten more examples of bubble feeding. Most of them, however, were too far away for us to be able to take good photos. During our

Unlike orcas and similar species, humpback whales have no teeth. They belong to the group of baleen whales. In their mouth there are hundreds of combs made of keratin which hang down from the upper jaw and are used to filter food from the water. Although their mouths can contain vast amounts of water, once they have expelled it there remains very little matter of any use between their combs. More agile prey can escape quickly, before the whale is able to close his mouth again. In the case of the fishing technique known as "bubble feeding", however, a group of whales will first drive a school of herring together. The whales emerge vertically from the depths in ever-decreasing spirals, slowly exhaling as they do so: this produces a dense net of air bubbles which keeps the herring together as if they were in a cage. There is no way of escaping this "prison". The whales shoot upwards with their mouths wide open. The herring floats directly into the whales' mouths.

I had already seen this form of fishing in a number of nature films, but on that day I was so nervous that I almost dropped my camera overboard.

All images: Observing humpback whales is one of the most impressive experiences on any Inside Passage Tour. The waters around Juneau are one of their favoured hunting grounds. Countless tours are offered. Very few whale watchers are lucky enough to see the famous phenomenon known as "bubble feeding".

Following double page: A tour boat directly in front of the vertical break-off edge of the South Sawyer Glacier in Tracy Arm.

return journey I almost forgot my bad luck with the leaping whale. I saw humpback whales fishing at close quarters – how could I fail to be satisfied with that?

In Auke Bay I said goodbye to Captain Harv and set off for Eagle River, where I planned to spend the night.

The beach lies some twenty kilometers (13 miles) north of Auke Bay. It was a beautifully quiet stretch of coastline. Bald eagles were sitting in the trees, the rivers were full of salmon, and from time to time you might come across a

black bear fishing. On that evening, however, it was the fine weather which encouraged me to head in that direction. The Coast Mountains were clearly visible. The sea had retreated; it was low tide.

I walked for a short distance along the shore and took pictures of the mountains, the coast, and the sunset. What a day it had been! After the last rays of sun had disappeared I crawled into my tent.

The next day I planned to head for the Tracy Arm.

Tracy Arm Fjord

The next morning it was pouring with rain. The weather can change here quickly. I packed up my tent and set off towards Juneau, although it was not exactly an attractive proposition to be making a trip up Tracy Arm during weather like that. Nonetheless I enquired in Juneau of a number of tour operators whether there was a space on their boat. "Yes, we have a spare place," said a friendly woman. I was not sure whether to be pleased or not. The weather was so bad that

you could scarcely see a hundred meters (328 feet) in front of you. I hesitated for a moment. The women in the office noticed my prevarication and explained to me that the ice on the glacier was a much more attractive blue color under a cloudy sky than when the sun was shining. Not quite convinced, I purchased a ticket. The little boat was full with about twenty other passengers, tourists from one of the cruise ships who have no time to wait for the weather to improve. Tracy Arm lies seventy kilometers south of Juneau. Two hours later we reached the entrance to the inlet. The boat slowed down. The twin glacier tongues in Tracy Arm produce so much ice that the icebergs are driven out of the inlet and into Stephens Passage. The captain headed towards a small iceberg. The ice was shimmering dark blue; the entire iceberg was almost transparent and blue all over. We sailed so close that I could almost touch the ice. The captain steered the boat once round the iceberg. I took one picture after

160

another. Such beautiful big icebergs do not drift out as far as this every year, said our captain, adding that this iceberg was one of the most beautiful ones to appear in recent years.

We continued on into the fjord. The landscape was breathtaking. The rock walls plunged steeply down into the sea from a height of several hundred meters. The water was as smooth as a mirror and shimmered in a wonderful shade of turquoise. We approached the steep, rocky banks. A black bear was searching the shore for shellfish. We got in as close as possible. All the passengers focused their cameras. The bear looked up briefly to see who was disturbing his peace, and then calmly continued his search. It was not exactly easy to get sharp pictures from the rocking boat. Thank goodness for picture stabilizers!

We headed further into the fjord. The temperature dropped and we could already feel the icy breath of the glacier. Tracy Arm is fifty kilometers long; the twin tongues of Sawyer Glacier lie

Top left: With a thundering noise a huge vertical section of the South Sawyer Glacier calves into the sea.

Bottom left: A black bear in search of food on the banks of Tracy Arm.

Top right: Some icebergs are so large that they are driven out of the bay into Stephens Passage.

Below right: The sea lions use the floating icebergs as a comfortable resting place.

161

at the end of the fjord and calve directly into the sea. The fjord was named after Benjamin Franklin Tracy, a general during the War of Secession. In 1980 the inlet, together with Endicott Arm, which runs parallel to it, was declared a Wilderness Area – one of the strictest class of protective areas – under the name "Tracy Arm-Fords Terror Wilderness". This means that 2,640 square kilometers (1019 square miles) are now under protection.

It had stopped raining, but the clouds were still very low. Then we saw the southern glacier tongue of Sawyer Glacier. A large number of small icebergs and ice floes were floating in front of the glacier. During my visit in 1997 we had been able to sail almost to the point where the glacier broke off into the sea. On this second visit that was impossible, because the entire bay was full of ice. It is known that Sawyer Glacier – like almost all the other glaciers in Alaska – is retreating, probably as a result of climate change. How long will we be able to continue to gaze in wonder at these gigantic rivers of ice?

On this occasion, however, the ice was shimmering in the most exquisite shades of blue. We could hear grinding, cracking sounds. Suddenly there was a loud bang and an entire wall of ice broke off into the sea. Fortunately at that very moment I had my camera focused on the edge of the glacier and was able to record the entire event.

The captain immediately turned the boat away, in order not to present it broadside to the flood wave. We all had to hold on as it hit the boat with massive force. And then, as the crowning glory of this event, the sun suddenly broke through the clouds. The sun's rays made the ice floes sparkle like diamonds. I took one picture after another. I was bitterly cold; I could no longer feel my fingers. I looked around and discovered that I was the only person left on deck. I had even missed lunch.

Only when the glacier tongue was no longer in view did I retreat below deck. When we turned into Stephens Passage, it started to rain again and did not stop until we reached Juneau.

Glacier Bay

The following days were a real trial of patience. The clouds hung heavily over Stephens Passage and the Gastineau Channel. It rained more or less continuously. I really wanted to fly to Glacier Bay National Park but I decided to wait for the weather to improve. After five days I became impatient. Surely the skies would clear at some point?

The next two days brought no improvement. I hiked along a few trails through the rainforest; I traveled over to Douglas Island, the island opposite Juneau; I photographed rocks, stones, shells. Eventually I ran out of things to photograph. Seven days of non-stop rain – I was on the verge of abandoning my planned trip to Glacier Bay. Ignoring all common sense I drove to the airport and chartered a plane for the next day to take me to Gustavus on the edge of Glacier Bay. From there it would only be a few kilometers to Bartlett Cove. There I could still wait for good weather.

The next day it was pouring again. With an uneasy feeling I clambered into the light aircraft. The flight from Juneau to Gustavus took about forty-five minutes, after which I took a taxi to Bartlett Cove – the springboard for trips to Glacier Bay National Park. There is a small National Park Center, as well as a lodge and a campsite. The tent area lies picturesquely in the middle of the rainforest, whose leaves form such a dense canopy that virtually no rain actually reaches the ground. The nearby lodge also has a delightful setting by the sea. Inside it was nice and warm, with good food and good coffee. The National Park Administration was on

the first floor. The Rangers were pleased to tell visitors all about the park, the fauna and the glaciers.

Left: The glaciers of Alaska are in retreat. In a few decades the calving glaciers of Glacier Bay may be a thing of the past.

Below: It is rare for the snow-covered mountains of Glacier Bay National Park to be so clearly visible.

Top right: A grizzly bear crossing a glacial stream in the National Park.

Right below: The Arctic goats seldom clamber far enough down the steep walls of rock for you to be able to photograph them at eye level.

Following double page: Evening colors above Lynn Channel.

Into the Park

Contrary to the forecast, after two days of rain the weather finally cleared. I was torn as to what I should do. Should I rent a kayak and go paddling for a few days or should I wait to see how the weather developed? I decided to start off by joining the guided tour to the park. A tourist boat leaves Bartlett Cove every day to visit the Bay. That morning the sky was absolutely cloudless. We were joined on board by a National Park Ranger, who told us a lot of interesting things about the park. The journey to the glaciers was a dream. The snow-capped mountains sparkled in the bright sunlight. We saw Steller sea lions, a threatened species, as well as puffins, sea otters and bald eagles. But the real highlight was the pack of wolves which the captain discovered on a lonely beach. It was a proper pack with a large number of wolf cubs, but unfortunately too far away to be able to take a decent photograph. We watched the creatures for a while, until they retreated into the undergrowth. Not many visitors are lucky enough to see wolves here. The captain assured us that it was a fortunate coincidence. I spent the entire trip to the glaciers on deck. The landscape looked wild and utterly untouched.

Towards noon we reached our main goal, Margerie Glacier. It is twenty-two kilometers (14 miles) long and up to 1.5 kilometers (1 mile) wide, and "flows" into the sea at the

163

end of Tarr Inlet. Even from a distance it presented a magnificent spectacle. In the background we could see the lofty peak of Mount Fairweather soaring heavenwards. At last we were right in front of the glacier. It creaked and groaned. Suddenly one of the passengers shouted: "Look, a grizzly just near the glacier!" And indeed it was – a grizzly bear was ambling along the beach. As quickly as I could, I got out my telescopic lens and began to take pictures. The bear looked as if it was about to cross a wild glacial stream. What a spectacle! Everyone on the boat had eyes only for the bear. Eventually it became too much for him and he disappeared behind the glacial scree.

But Margerie Glacier presented us with another spectacle too: a huge lump of ice broke off and crashed into the water.

The return trip was uneventful. We "only" saw a few sea otters and bald eagles, and at 6 p.m. the boat re-entered Bartlett Cove. The following days I wanted to take the kayak out into the Bay. But the next day brought an unpleasant surprise: the weather had changed yet again. It was raining and the clouds hung low in the sky. I had just four days left before I had to return to Juneau. Two days of fine weather would be suf-

Above: The rain has stopped. At Eagle Beach north of Juneau the sea has retreated and left picturesque tidal pools behind.

Top right and below: The Arctic terns defend their nests against all invaders with furious attacks.

Following double page: When the clouds are particularly low and everything becomes blurred, the landscape of southeast Alaska can look like a painting – as here on Douglas Island.

ficient for me to take a few good pictures. But the next four days it would probably not stop raining the whole time. One of the National Park Rangers said that fine weather only occurred there, statistically speaking, on about one or two days every month. After waiting for another four days I clambered back into the aircraft which took me back to Juneau. The next time I would come for two weeks; then it would

work out. Reluctantly I took leave of Glacier Bay. It was my third visit and in spite of the weather problems one of my best.

The next day it was pouring yet again. I was pleased that I would be catching the ferry to Haines the following day. The next day found me sitting at the ferry terminal, waiting for the ship. The weather was fine, with not a cloud in the blue sky.

Glacier Bay National Park

When the Russian explorer Alexei Ilyich Chirikov arrived in 1741, he saw nothing but ice. At that time, the entire bay was still completely covered with ice. And then in 1794, when the famous George Vancouver explored the region, it was impossible to sail into the bay, because the ice sheet was still too thick.

It was the famous natural scientist John Muir, who first told the world about the natural wonder of Glacier Bay. He visited the area in 1879. By this point the glaciers had retreated seventy-seven kilometers (forty-eight miles), far enough to permit him to sail into the bay. Nowhere else in the world did ice retreat to this extent. With the assistance of local guides, John Muir studied the glaciers and mapped the region for the US government. He was fascinated by its untamed nature. Muir made seven long journeys to Alaska and began writing scientific and travel reports which were published throughout the country and aroused much interest. By the end of the 1880s the first tourists had visited the region in order to experience the magnificent sight of Glacier Bay first hand. What would John Muir think if he could see Glacier Bay today? Since then, the glaciers have retreated still farther, so that today the bay is virtually ice-free.

Of the more than 200 glaciers which lie within the boundaries of today's National Park, sixteen calve into the sea. The area became a National Monument in 1925, no doubt due to John Muir, whose reports and tales greatly influenced the US president of the time, Theodore Roosevelt. In 1980 Glacier Bay was declared a National Park and in 1992 it was entered into UNESCO's list of World Heritage sites. Today, more than 350,000 tourists visit the park each year. Glacier Bay National Park is thus one of the most popular travel destinations in North America. The visitor will discover such highlights as spectacular glaciers which calve into the sea and a picturesque mountain and fjord landscape surmounted by Mount Fairweather (4600 meters/ 1748 feet), the highest peak. The park's fauna is unique. It is the habitat of humpback whales,

orcas, grey whales, dolphins, grizzlies, black bears, wolves, bald eagles, sea otters, sea lions and seals.

Scientists estimate that the park is also home to more than 240 avian species and more than 200 fish species. With luck you may even see the rare glacier bear, a sub-species of the black bear with lighter, blue-grey shimmering fur. Apart from Bartlett Cove there are no footpaths in the entire park. Visitors have only themselves and their own resources to rely on. The best way of exploring the park is by kayak, but you must be able to put up with long periods of bad weather. It is essential to have a certain amount of wilderness experience if you want to explore the park on your own.

From Juneau to Skagway
Trail of the Fortune Hunters

He loved the life, the deep arctic winter, the silent wilderness, the unending snow-surface unpressed by the foot of any man. About him towered icy peaks unnamed and uncharted. (...) He loved it all, the day's toil, the bickering wolf-dogs, the making of the camp in the long twilight, the leaping stars overhead and the flaming pageant of the aurora borealis.

Jack London (1876–1916), Smoke Bellew, 1912

Eagles and Gold

The weather was magnificent. The sun was shining in a cloudless sky. It was the first time that I was traveling from Juneau to Haines on a fine day. The journey through the Lynn Canal is probably one of the most scenic sections of the entire Inside Passage.

The *Matanuska* left Auke Bay. Once again I had a breathtaking view of Mendenhall Glacier and the Juneau Icefield. After about an hour's traveling we were in the middle of the Lynn Canal. The view is simply grandiose. To the left and right, craggy, snow-capped mountains rise up into the blue sky. In many places, massive glacier tongues creep down into the valley. The mountains, with their ridges and peaks, reminded me very much of the coast of Norway. Very few passengers were below deck. Even locals who have traveled this route hundreds of times were standing on the upper deck and admiring the magnificent landscape in the sunlight.

The Lynn Canal extends about 130 kilometers (78 miles) from Icy Strait in the south to Skagway in the north. On a day like this it was difficult to imagine that this particular stretch of water is in fact quite hazardous. Numerous ships have fallen victim to its treacherous winds. The high mountains have the same effect as a wind tunnel. Winds can reach speeds of up to 130 kph/ 81 mph here. They are especially dangerous when they whip up the incoming tide. It was this combination of circumstances that led to the worst shipping accident on the Pacific Northwest coast. In 1918 the *Princess Sophia* ran aground during a severe storm on the Vanderbilt Reef, and all 343 passengers drowned.

Halfway to Haines we passed the Eldred Rock Light Station, one of the picture-postcard images of the Inside Passage. The lighthouse is the oldest of its kind in Alaska. It was put into operation in 1906, but has not been manned for some years now. I have sailed past it at least five times, but on each occasion the weather was so bad that I was unable to take a photo. This time the red roof was glowing in the sunlight, and in the background, the snow-capped mountain peaks soared heavenwards – what more could a photographer wish for?

After six hours, Haines came into view. It is one of the few places in southeast Alaska which is linked to the road network. The Haines Highway is 246 kilometers (154 miles) long and leads from Haines through a picturesque mountain landscape to Haines Junction in the Yukon Territory, across the border in Canada, where it joins the famous Alaska Highway.

In spite of its road connections, Haines is a sleepy little place. Today, 2,500 inhabitants live here at the end of the Chilkat Valley at the foot of the Takhinska Mountains.

Long before the "white man" settled here, the Tlingit lived in the Chilkat Valley. They called the place where Haines now lies *Dei-Shu* – The End of the Trail.

The Tlingit used to live in several villages along the Chilkat River. Today, the only settlement left is Klukwan, some forty kilometers (25 miles) north of Haines. Since the natural resources in the region provided everything they needed in abundance, the Chilkat, as this particular group of Tlingit was called, had plenty of time to spend on art and crafts. The famous, beautifully woven Chilkat blankets are sold for high prices

to this day. The Tlingit and the European explorers first met in 1741, when a Russian ship anchored near Haines. Thereupon the Russians and Indians developed a lively trade in furs. In 1879, Samuel Hall Young was the first missionary to reach the region. He was searching for a suitable place to build a school and a mission station. The estuary of the Chilkat River, the present-day location of Haines, proved ideal for his purpose. As a result of the frontier dispute between the United States and Canada, the US

Previous double page: The Cathedral Peaks in the first light of morning

Left: What a location: framed by the majestic Chilkat Mountains lies historic Fort Seward, directly at the end of the Chilkat Valley.

Bottom left: On fine days the six-hour journey through Lynn Channel (130 kilometers/ 81 miles) on one of the ferries of the Alaska Marine Highway System is a true feast for the eyes.

Right below: Winter on Chilkat Inlet. The receding tide has revealed bizarre ice formations.

Army built a military base here between 1902 and 1904. Until World War Two, Fort William H. Seward was the only permanently manned military base in Alaska. In 1947 a group of war veterans purchased the fort. They wanted to set up an artists' colony – which they partially succeeded with.

Today the white wooden cottages of Fort William H. Seward are all privately owned and are one of the main attractions of the village. They have been transformed into little hotels, restaurants, galleries and shops. The inhabitants earn their living primarily from fishing and tourism.

What I particularly like about Haines is its authentic natural charm, which it possibly owes to the fact that it does not lie on the main route followed by the cruise liners. Unlike Ketchikan or Skagway, you will find in the shops in Haines virtually no kitschy tourist souvenirs, but rather everyday necessities, and here and then a wonderful piece of craftsmanship.

177

A Picturesque Landscape

Haines lies on a peninsula between Chilkat and Chilkoot Inlet, surrounded by the snow-capped mountains of the Chilkat Range which predestine Haines as a center for outdoor activities. The Mount Ripinsky Trail begins right in town; it will take you about three hours to walk to the summit, which lies at almost 1,200 meters (3936 feet). You will be rewarded by a magnificent view of the Takhinska Mountains in the

west and Chilkat and Chilkoot Inlet in the south. To the north rise the mighty Takshanuk Mountains. However, if you prefer fishing, you will find that the Chilkoot River provides ideal conditions near the lake of the same name. Every year, thousands of salmon head upstream. This is regarded as being one of the best fishing locations in the whole of southeast Alaska. The Chilkoot River Road leads from Haines some 17 kilometers (11 miles) to the Chilkoot Lake State Recreation Site, where in

summer the competition is fierce of the best angling sites. From early summer to late fall in mid-October, four major salmon migrations take place on the river. However, anglers should always keep an eye on their surroundings, because large numbers of salmon also attract grizzly bears. I have experienced myself how a bear snatched away an angler's catch. In retrospect I can't help smiling at the scene, but it was not without danger at the time. There is a magnificent camp site by Chilkoot Lake; I have always used it as my overnight base during my visits to Haines. Countless bald eagles sit in the trees around the camp site, waiting patiently for their share of the prey.

The Chilkat State Park is also worth a visit. It lies some twelve kilometers (8 miles) south of Haines on the Mud Bay Road, directly on the peninsula which separates Chilkoot Inlet from Chilkat Inlet. Even from the road there is a breathtaking view across Chilkat Inlet to the Chilkat Mountains. The park provides a habitat

Top left: In January the Chilkat Valley lies beneath a deep layer of snow.

Bottom left: If you drive a few miles into the interior on the Haines Highway, you will find yourself in a unique high-mountain landscape.

Top right: A fly fisher tries his luck on the Chilkoot River.

Right above: Up to three thousand bald eagles gather in November and December in the Chilkat Valley, where they eat their fill on salmon yet again. Each tree is occupied by the majestic birds.

179

All images: In winter the Chilkat Valley provides a unique opportunity to observe the heraldic bird of the United States, the bald eagle, at close quarters. A late salmon migration attracts eagles from the remotest corners of Alaska and Canada to this remarkable place. The Chilkat Bald Eagle Preserve was established in 1982 in order to protect this natural spectacle.

for moose and black bears which I have encountered on every occasion whenever I have followed one of the three trails in the park. The route I consider to be the most attractive leads up Mount Riley (540 meters/ 1771 feet). A little path winds up the mountain over a distance of 4.5 kilometers (3 miles) through an unspoiled forest. You will hardly see a soul. You should allow about an hour and a half for the 500-meter (1640 feet) climb. You will be rewarded with a spectacular view of the two inlets and the snow-capped mountains of the surroundings.

Haines is also the starting point for a trip into the Glacier Bay National Park, which is only a short distance away by seaplane. Several firms in the village offer round trips by plane above the spectacular mountains and glaciers of the park.

Even if the weather is bad, Haines provides enough opportunities for activity. In the Alaska Indian Arts Center, which lies directly beside the historic Fort Seward, you can watch how the exquisite Tlingit screen prints are made. The artists who carve the famous totem poles are also here. Onlookers are welcome and of course the artworks are also for sale, although the prices are not particularly low.

Sheldon Museum and Cultural Center is devoted to the culture of the Chilkat as well as the history of Haines and the settlement of the region by the European immigrants.

Those who wish to experience Indian culture at close hand should visit the Chilkat Dancers in the Storytelling Theater. In their dances they revive the old stories and legends of the Tlingit. Of particular interest are the artistically carved wooden masks and the elaborately decorated tradition costumes which the actors wear on stage. The Storytelling Theater is located in the Totem Village Tribal House in old Fort William H. Seward.

A Winter Tour into the Valley of Eagles

If you drive into the Chilkat Valley in summer from the north, you will not realize at first what a special place you are entering. At some point, signs appear along the roadside bearing the message "Chilkat Bald Eagle Preserve". I can still remember my first visit here eleven years ago. When I saw the sign I immediately stopped and searched the valley of the Chilkat River with my binoculars, hoping to see eagles. But I could not see any. Disappointed, I climbed back into the car and drove on.

Only later did I learn that I had been there at the wrong time entirely. In winter, between November and January, you can experience a unique natural spectacle seen nowhere else on Earth beside the Chilkat River.

The Chilkat Bald Eagle Preserve was established in 1982, in order to protect the largest colony of bald eagles in the world. The protected area extends over a total of 194 square kilometers (75 square miles). Between November and January, more than 3,000 bald eagles gather by the Chilkat River in order to eat their fill during Alaska's last salmon migration. The peak occurs in November. The trees and the entire river bed are simply crowded with eagles. They even migrate all the way from Washington State. Why does it happen? Warm-water springs from the earth's core keep this stretch of river north of Haines free of ice, even in winter. The salmon take advantage of this last opportunity for a final, large-scale migration. Because of its salmon stocks the Tlingit call the river *Jilkáat Heeni*, which means approximately "the basket for stocks of salmon in winter."

For ten years this magical place had haunted me, until, in winter 2007, I was finally able to visit the Chilkat Bald Eagle Preserve. Most eagles are here from the end of October to the

end of November; from December onwards their numbers decrease, but there are still plenty to see. I had planned to visit the region in January, since there would be fewer tourists than in November and I would have a better chance of photographing the eagles in attractive winter surroundings.

Even the drive from Haines Junction along the Haines Highway was an experience. The countryside was covered in snow and the mountains

Top left: A picture which symbolizes Alaska for me: a bald eagle against the awe-inspiring backdrop of the snow-covered Chilkat Mountains.
Bottom and right (both): It is rare for the weather in Haines and surroundings to be as good as this. Thick clouds and mist usually permit you only to guess at the magnificent mountain scenery. In winter the cloud cover cleared for a couple of days and the landscape showed itself in its best light.

looked like white giants, with not a single stone or rock to be recognized. At this season you will be virtually alone. On the entire route between Haines Junction and the Canadian-US border, I saw only one other car. The closer I got to the coast, the higher the mountains appeared. The temperature also rose slowly. When I crossed the border from Canada to the US, the snow was so high that from the road you could not see a thing beyond the vast heaps of snow. I slowly followed the bends of the Haines Highway down into the valley, until I finally reached the Chilkat Bald Eagle Preserve. The landscape was covered in hoar frost, and on virtually every tree there sat a group of bald eagles.

I parked my car on one of the marked spaces, slowly climbed out, put up my tripod and started to take pictures. I had never seen so many bald eagles in a single place. There were

even twenty to thirty eagles sitting on the river bank. In November, when the invasion of birds reaches its zenith, the entire valley is full of eagles – and unfortunately also full of people. Then there is no chance of getting a hotel room: tourists and photographers from all over the globe lay siege to the village.

This time, however, I had no difficulty finding a hotel room in Haines. I spent most of the next four days observing and photographing the eagles. Unfortunately the weather was very bad at first; the clouds were low and it kept on snowing. But on the fifth day the skies finally cleared and the sun struggled to break through the morning mist. I could slowly make out the silhouettes of the mountains. The morning light bathed the Chilkat Valley and the surrounding mountains in an orange light. I almost forgot the eagles, the landscape was so lovely. The weather held for two days. I photographed

eagles, snow-covered mountains, stranded icebergs, snowy trees... After a week I had to return to Canada and the Yukon Territory. When I set off early in the morning it was still dark. The full moon bathed the Chilkat Valley in a ghostly light. For the last time I drove past the Chilkat Bald Eagle Preserve. High up in the crown of a tree I spotted an eagle and stopped.

From where I was standing he was directly in front of the full moon. I could not ignore the opportunity – I mounted my camera on the tripod again and took one picture after another. Eventually the bird had had enough and flew away. I reached Haines Junction late that evening. It was good that I had decided to come in January.

To Skagway – On the Trail of Gold Diggers and Fortune Hunters

This time my visit to Haines was in July, and I was sitting at the ferry terminal, waiting for my ferry to Skagway. I had originally toyed with the

Above: A solitary fishing cutter in Chilkoot Inlet near Haines. Even in summer, the mountains in the background are covered in snow.

Top right: The Eldred Rock Light Station, halfway between Juneau and Haines. The lighthouse is the oldest of its kind in Alaska.

Right above: Trumpeter swans in the Chilkat Valley in winter.

thought of traveling to Skagway via the land route, but then the prospect of 580 kilometers (363 miles) through Canada's Yukon Territory put me off. By sea, Skagway is only about twenty kilometers (13 miles) from Haines; it lies idyllically at the end of Taiya Inlet, a branch of the Lynn Canal. The journey by boat only takes about an hour. By road, on the other hand, you

would need at least an entire day. For those with time to spare, however, the trip via the Haines Highway, the Alaska Highway and then the Klondike Highway is highly recommended. The journey through the wild mountain scenery of the Tatshenshini-Alsek Provincial Park and the Kluane National Park is simply breathtaking. And Whitehorse, the capital of the Yukon

Previous double page: The last swirls of mist are clearing. The first light of morning bathes the snowy Chilkat Valley in golden light.

Left below: In Jack London's time Skagway was considered to be a wild, lawless place. Today it keeps its disreputable image alive only to please the tourists.

Bottom left: In the Alaska Indian Arts Center in historic Fort Seward you can watch Indian artists at work.

Center: Skagway looks like a film set of a town in the Wild West. It is lively and crowded in summer, but in winter it resembles a ghost town.

Top right: In the Storytelling Theater in Haines (Fort Seward) the old stories of the Tlingit people live on.

Territory, has retained the charm of an outpost of civilization.

The ferry journey to Skagway during the early afternoon was scenically attractive, but without the many highlights of the trip along the Lynn Canal. Before long the town came into view, one of the bastions of the cruise ship program. The *Leconte* berthed at the terminal and shortly afterwards I drove my car off the ferry. Two large cruise liners were anchored in the harbor. When I turned into the main street I was pleasantly surprised. The entire town may live off tourism, but it still has flair. The wooden houses have been retained in the original style of the turn of the last century. I could have felt that I had been transported back to the period of economic expansion – had it not been for the

numerous souvenir shops and the thousands of tourists milling through the streets. More than 150,000 tourists visit Skagway every year. The town has put on its Sunday best for its visitors. The numerous old houses have been carefully renovated and now form part of the Klondike Gold Rush National Historical Park. What must it have been like here 110 years ago, when the legendary gangster "Soapy" Smith struck terror into people's hearts and 10,000 gold prospectors lived in Skagway?

After two hours in the bustle I had had enough. I set off towards Dyea and found myself wondering what would be left of the place. A small, bumpy track led from Skagway to the place where Dyea once stood. I spent half an hour searching in vain until I realized that the hand-

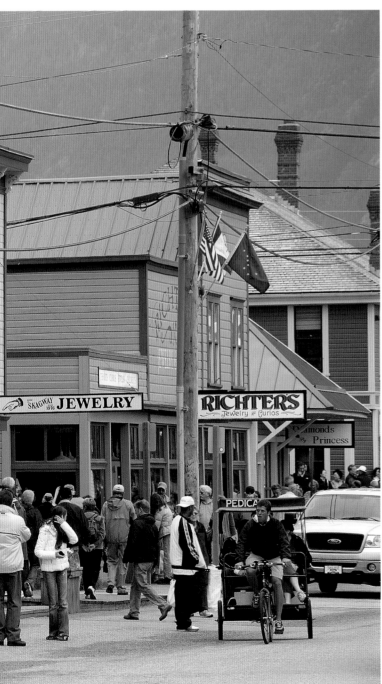

turers. If you want to follow the 53-kilometer (33-mile) trail to the end you should allow three to five days and you should be reasonably fit and have a certain amount of wilderness and mountain experience. The route is not very challenging as mountain treks go, but sudden changes in the weather can make life difficult. After traversing the 53 kilometers (33 miles) you will reach Lake Bennett – the destination for the travellers in those days. The gold prospectors who got this far had not covered even a quarter of the route to Dawson City. I hiked only the first fifteen kilometers (9 miles) along the river and admired the relics of the Gold-Rush era. At the "Golden Stairs", however, I turned round and headed back to the car.

That evening I sat in my tent and read Jack London's *Alaska Kid*. In it, the writer describes the route along the Chilkoot Trail. Jack London was one of the many adventurers who wanted to get rich on the Klondike and who failed miserably. He wrote about his impressions of his time in Alaska and Canada not only in *Smoke Bellew*, but also in *White Fang* and *The Call of the Wild*.

Farewell

The next morning it was time for me to leave Skagway, the Inside Passage, the rainforest. The past weeks had been strenuous and nerve-racking, but above all wonderful – indescribable, unique. I had watched humpback whales "bubble feeding" and had seen the legendary spirit bear; I had photographed brown and black bears catching salmon at close quarters and experienced calving glaciers. I had hiked through a unique rainforest. From Dyea I took the bumpy road back to Skagway. I treated myself to a hearty breakfast in Skagway in order to postpone my departure for a short while. And then it was time. I left the town and set off

ful of ruined wooden shacks in the forest were all that remained of Dyea. It seemed almost incredible that at one time up to 10,000 people had lived here. I strolled through the forest and discovered a graveyard from the old gold-prospecting era. "E.T. Hutton, Portland, Oregon, died on April 3, 1898, in an avalanche" was the inscription on one of the graves. How many gold prospectors had to pay for their longing for fortune and wealth with their life?

Not far from the ruined houses I found the start of the famous Chilkoot Trail. One hundred years ago, the people would have been pleased to have been spared the arduous journey; today, tourists from all over the world come to trek along the route taken by the gold prospectors of yore. The path leads through spectacular mountain scenery. Relics of the old gold-prospecting days dot the sides of the path every now and then. Originally, the trail follows the Taiya River before leaving the canyon. A good twenty kilometers (13 miles) further on, you reach the "Golden Stairs", which over a century ago proved the Waterloo of so many of the adven-

All images: If you follow the Klondike Highway from Skagway for a few miles into the interior you will find yourself in a wild mountain landscape. You may even be lucky enough to see moose or perhaps a red fox.
Following double page: The mountains of Tatshenshini-Alsek Provincial Park can only be explored on hikes lasting for several days.

190

along the Klondike Highway in the direction of the Canadian border. The sun was shining in a cloudless sky. Somehow the weather seemed totally inappropriate for my low spirits. How long would this paradise be able to survive? Climate change and all its consequences can already be seen here. Everywhere is getting warmer all the time. The glaciers of Alaska, once so vast, are disappearing at top speed. The water temperatures are rising. What effect will that have on the salmon migrations, which are regarded as the lifeblood of the Inside Passage?

New animal species will migrate from the south and drive out many of the local species. We are in a position to prevent more serious damage. Only if we act immediately and slow down our insatiable thirst for energy will it be possible to change course. Perhaps it is necessary to have seen this unique natural paradise on the northwest coast of North America with one's own eyes, to have smelt the rainforest, to have observed the bears catching salmon, to be able to comprehend what it will really mean if the paradise is destroyed.

That evening I sat in front of my tent amid the magnificent mountain scenery of Kluane National Park the Yukon Territory of Canada. The sky was completely clear. In the heavens a pale green arc appeared; the Aurora Borealis was beginning. After about ten minutes the Northern Lights illuminated the heavens in beautiful shades of green. How I love this country, the north, Alaska, Canada! I was already looking forward to the next weeks. My journey was to take me northward to the Arctic Circle. But that is another story!

The Gold Rush on the Klondike River

It all began in 1896. "Gold, gold!" was the cry that echoed round the world. The gold prospectors John Carmacks, Charlie Tagish and Jim Skookum had found gold by the Klondike River, a tributary of the Yukon River. The news of vast gold deposits in the Yukon spread across the country like wildfire. From then on there was no stopping it. Thousands of fortune-hunters from all over the world headed for the Klondike River. Although the gold was found in the neighboring Yukon Territory, it had a dramatic effect on many small communities along the Inside Passage. The sea route through the Passage was the easiest way of reaching the far north. Hundreds of thousands of gold prospectors set off for a virtually undeveloped region which had hitherto been of little or no interest to the rest of the world. The ships headed for Dyea and Skagway. These two little towns, only a few kilometers apart, had been insignificant Indian settlements until that point. All that changed overnight, for it was from here that the gold prospectors now started their long march across the mountains into the neighbouring Yukon Territory. Within a short time, more than 10,000 people had gathered in Dyea and Skagway.

It was in the Tlingit settlement of Dyea that the notorious Chilkoot Trail began; and it was in Skagway that the fortune hunters gathered before crossing the White Pass into Canada. Both trails led to Lake Bennett, at which point the prospectors continued northward by boat or on a raft.

The Chilkoot Trail and the White Pass were both old Tlingit trading routes. As early as 1887, William "Buddy" Moore had suspected that there was gold to be found in the Yukon Territory. The former steamship captain had learned that geologically similar regions of South America and Mexico also contained gold deposits. In order to find the best route across the mountains he joined an expedition into the border area and drew a route. The foundation for what would later become the route of the White Pass Railroad was determined.

The fortune hunters faced incredible hardship after their arrival. The Canadian border guards refused to allow the gold prospectors to enter the country unless they carried sufficient food supplies for a year. That was not just a means of harassment; the Canadians were afraid that the gold prospectors would die of hunger en

route – or that lack of food would lead to a sharp rise in theft and crime. They needed a tonne of supplies and equipment, including 500 pounds of flour, 100 pounds of sugar and 500 candles. Very few of the gold prospectors could afford porters or a horse and so they had to make several journeys across the passes in order to transport all their supplies. The Royal Canadian Mounted Police checked very carefully to make sure that no one crossed the border without food. The harsh winters, cold and avalanches were additional sources of hardship for the men and women.

The pictures of the long queues of fortune hunters struggling up the legendary "Golden Stairs" of the Chilkoot Pass are world famous. For the last few kilometers, more than 1500 steps hewn into the ice led up to the pass in those days. The hikers had to walk a distance of over fifty kilometers (31 miles). Once they had crossed the pass, they still had another 500 kilometers (313 miles) to go.

Dyea slowly lost its importance as increasingly large ships started to arrive from the south. The harbor there was not deep enough for the boats to berth. Skagway, by contrast, blossomed into a golden age which would never be repeated. In 1897 to 1898 the number of inhabitants grew rapidly from a few hundred to over 10,000. Skagway was thus not only Alaska's largest town – it was also the most lawless place in the state. Shootings and prostitution were part of the everyday routine.

The most famous gangster in town was Jefferson Randolph "Soapy" Smith, who ruled the town with his Skagway Military Company and terrorized the citizens. He appeared to be a gentleman with good manners and an open ear for the sufferings of the poor, but if you looked below the surface it was clear that he was only concerned to fill his own pockets, and that he lied and deceived everyone. He and his wild gang were so powerful and so feared that no one dared to resist him. The rule of "Soapy" Smith lasted until July 8, 1898 when his rival Frank Reid shot him on the street.

In 1898 the tracks were laid for a 20-kilometer (13-mile) long steam railroad up to the White Pass. The railroad was for those who could afford to use it – and for them it was an enormous saving in time and energy. Most of the poor prospectors had to continue to drag their provisions up the pass under great suffering. Construction on a proper railroad for the White Pass began in September 1898, sealing the fate of Dyea, the other starting point for the journey to the goldfields. And yet, by 1899 it was all over. The fortune hunters had moved on; new finds of gold by the Bering Strait near Nome in Alaska lured them away. Dyea collapsed completely and Skagway shrank back almost to its original size.

Today some 800 inhabitants live there year round; it is only in the summer months that the population "explodes" to almost 2000. Most are seasonal workers who are hired to look after the tourists on the cruise chips. Many tourists take advantage of the opportunity to make a trip up the White Pass in the historic railroad. The route travels through magnificent, wild high mountain scenery. Today, however, the trains only run for the tourists and they turn back to Skagway again as soon as they have reached the White Pass.

195

Taking photographs

Taking photographs

Thirteen years ago, when I traveled to Alaska for the first time, I took photos for pleasure – for my own use. I spent seven weeks in the far north, went hiking and studied the landscape and the animals. It was a period of "slow traveling" during which I got to know the land. When I visit Alaska these days it is to take photographs for specific projects which (unfortunately) have to earn money. This means that many things have changed; above all, I have to cope with the pressure of having to produce good – printable – pictures, of being constantly in conflict with adverse weather and lighting conditions or "obstinate" wild animals which simply refuse to present themselves in a photogenic pose. Sometimes I wonder whether this constant eye on the viewfinder, the pressure to get a good photo, affects the way I see nature and the magnificent landscapes. It may indeed be so – at least to a certain extent – but looking at nature through the camera also sharpens one's awareness of the country or regions through which one is traveling. Sometimes the camera even opens the door to a world which others do not see at all. Because I am constantly searching for motifs for my photos I get up when others are still asleep in bed or in their tent. I find places that "normal travelers" will never come across. And yet all the time I have to force myself to slow down, to simply stop and look, to allow the impressions to sink in, to enjoy what I see instead of simply making use of it.

The most important thing is to have a positive attitude to the "motif", whatever it may be. I would even go so far as to say that only those who feel a close affinity with the project in hand, which represents the content of their job, who identify with the country, the people and the natural surroundings, will manage to take really good photos. Thirteen years ago I fell in love with the far north and since then I have returned almost every year. I hope that this deep affection for the country is reflected in my pictures.

A Few Technical Details

The Inside Passage was the first photographic project that I carried out almost entirely with a digital camera. In this book, we have used only a handful of slides from the old era of analogue (or film) photography. Ten years ago I traveled to Alaska with 300 slide films in my luggage; today I travel with a laptop, a portable cache and lots of memory sticks.

Digital photography is not only a blessing; it is also a curse at the same time. A blessing because I can check on my computer screen immediately what the picture I have just taken really looks like, because I can change the ASA setting on my camera as required, because I cannot run out of film (which used to happen regularly) and because the pictorial quality of a 13-megapixel camera is superior to that of any small-format slide film. And a curse because you become an "energy junkie", constantly in search of power sources for batteries and computer, because a congenial supper at night has to be sacrificed to the downloading of data and the examination of photographs.

Initially I was a bit concerned as to whether my sensitive digital cameras would stand up to the damp climate of the Inside Passage. My fears were groundless, however. I photographed with three Canon EOS-5-D cameras which never let me down. Even during continuous rain the cameras never failed to function; of course, I took care to protect them against damp at all times. It is important to have three cameras on long, expensive journeys, because I have often experienced that one or the other of them might malfunction temporarily. As far as lenses are concerned, I mostly used a 4/17-40mm, a 2.8/70-200mm zoom and a 2.8/300mm. Sensitive lenses are a must in the dark rainforest, in order to obtain high-quality shots of animals. I was constantly surprised at the excellent quality of the digital photos taken with high ASA settings. Even pictures taken with 1000 ASA were wonderfully fine-grained and full of detail. Without these new possibilities of digital photography some of my animal shots would not have been successful.

Power is a big problem in the wilderness. Most digital cameras today run on batteries which, however, must be recharged regularly. In order to cope with this problem I always took with me a large number of fully charged batteries which mostly just about kept me going. Data storage also requires energy. Here I recommend the use of small, portable caches which can be used either with rechargeable or with normal throw-away batteries.

None of the pictures in this book was digitally manipulated. That is to say, nothing was added and nothing was retouched. In some cases the color values were corrected slightly and the white balance (color temperature) was adjusted.

Index

Imprint / Acknowledgements

See our full listing of books at
www.bucher-publishing.com

Translation: Jane Michael, Munich, Germany
Proofreading: Elizabeth Harcourt, Picton,
Canada
Product management for the English edition:
Dr. Birgit Kneip
Product management for the German edition:
Susanne Caesar
Design: graphitecture book, Rosenheim, Germany
Repro: Repro Ludwig, Zell am See, Austria
Jacket design: Melanie Sandbiller, Munich,
Germany; photos: Bernd Römmelt
Cartography: Astrid Fischer-Leitl, Munich,
Germany
Production: Bettina Schippel
Printed in Italy by Printer Trento

This work has been carefully researched by the
author and kept up to date as well as checked
by the publisher for coherence. However, the
publishing house can assume no liability for
the accuracy of the data contained herein.
We are always grateful for suggestions and
advice. Please send your comments to:
C.J. Bucher Publishing, Product Management
Infanteriestrasse 11 A, 80797 Munich
Germany
e-mail: editorial@bucher-publishing.com

Credits: Library of Congress Washington,
pp 32/33, 195; all others: Bernd Römmelt

Acknowledgements:
My special thanks to my family for supporting
me all the time and being happy when I came
back healthy. I would also like to thank
Susanne Caesar from Bruckmann Verlag,
believing in the project from the beginning.
Thanks also to Birgit Kneip for the careful edi-
tion of my texts. Thanks to Vernon Craig from
the Alaska Marine Highway System for sup-
porting my journeys, and to Trish and Eric
from Ocean Adventures for showing me the
Kermode bear. Thanks to Tyson and Bill
Mackay from Mackay Whale Watching for sup-
porting me in order to get photos of orcas.
Furthermore I would like to thank Sonya
Mayer, Michael Lechner, Gaby and Bernhard
Fichtl, Marcus Klotzsche, Ron Schreiber, Ida
Newton, Paul Lange, Melka Meltzer, Sabine
Mertens and Rainer Lohmann.

ISBN 978-3-7658-1642-0